Praise for Sacred

"Anni Daulter and Niki Dewart offer moms a collection of blessings. These pages are a weaving of word medicine, inspirati...on, and celebration. Mothers, buckle your seat belts. Read, sing, scribble, sketch, dance, dare to begin this journey. It goes one way, toward your own inner knowing."

—*Robin Lim,* midwife, founder of Yayasan Bumi Sehat (Healthy Mother Earth Foundation), and CNN 2011 Hero of the Year

"What a gorgeous, life-changing invitation this book is for anyone on the journey of growing into and through motherhood. It also uniquely embodies deep feminine wisdom—which we all share—and invites us to drink deeply at that source. A true gift!"

—*Rahima Baldwin Dancy,* midwife and author of *You Are Your Child's First Teacher*

"Sacred Motherhood is a heroine's journey, illuminating the wisdom of the divine feminine. Beginning with 'The Call,' women are invited to follow a sensory-rich rhythm through the seasons, accompanied by essential allies—Trust, Intuition, Sisterhood, and more—and offered gentle opportunities for healing along the way. Anni and Niki have created an exquisite guide and gift, adorned with sacred body beauty, grounded in messy truth, and languaged with love. This book is a 'boon' and a celebration."

—*Janet Lucy,* author of *Moon Mother, Moon Daughter*

"Of course we are grateful for our children, but so often we are overrun with the chaos of the day-to-day that we don't have the bandwidth to pause and reflect on this beautiful journey. Sacred Motherhood not only reminds us, but also gives us tools to elevate our thinking and bring us into a nurturing space for both our children and ourselves. This book has a permanent place on my bedside table!"

—*Kim Graham-Nye,* mother and cofounder of gDiapers

Sacred Motherhood

Sacred Motherhood

An Inspirational Guide and Journal for
Mindfully Mothering Children of All Ages

ANNI DAULTER AND NIKI DEWART

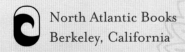

North Atlantic Books
Berkeley, California

Published by
North Atlantic Books
Berkeley, California

Cover photo by Jade Beall
Cover and book design by Claudia Smelser
Printed in Canada

Sacred Motherhood: An Inspirational Guide and Journal for Mindfully Mothering Children of All Ages is sponsored and published by the Society for the Study of Native Arts and Sciences (dba North Atlantic Books), an educational nonprofit based in Berkeley, California, that collaborates with partners to develop cross-cultural perspectives, nurture holistic views of art, science, the humanities, and healing, and seed personal and global transformation by publishing work on the relationship of body, spirit, and nature.

North Atlantic Books' publications are available through most bookstores. For further information, visit our website at www.northatlanticbooks.com or call 800-733-3000.

LIBRARY OF CONGRESS CATALOGING-IN-PUBLICATION DATA

Names: Daulter, Anni, author. | Dewart, Niki, 1973- author.
Title: Sacred motherhood : an inspirational guide and journal for mindfully mothering children of all ages / Anni Daulter & Niki Dewart.
Description: Berkeley, California : North Atlantic Books, [2015]
Identifiers: LCCN 2015051031 | ISBN 9781623170042 (paperback)
Subjects: LCSH: Motherhood—Religious aspects. | Mothers. | Spiritual life. | Mother goddesses. | BISAC: FAMILY & RELATIONSHIPS / Parenting / Motherhood. | SELF-HELP / Personal Growth / Happiness. | BODY, MIND & SPIRIT / Healing / General.
Classification: LCC BL625.68 .D38 2015 | DDC 204/.41—dc23
LC record available at http://lccn.loc.gov/2015051031

2 3 4 5 6 7 8 9 VERSA 23 22 21 20 19 18

To all women everywhere who long for beauty, passion, inspiration, and sisterhood amidst the miracles and madness of the mothering years. To our children—Afton, Bodhi, Haven, Lotus, River, Story, and Zoë—who have called us to the sacred path of motherhood.

To my husband, Tim, for lovingly supporting me through my journey as a mother, our journey as parents, and our journey as beloved partners.

ᐤ ANNI

To my soulmate, Steve, who has held a deep heart-space for me to birth this book and our sacred family.

ᐤ NIKI

CONTENTS

$\mathcal{I}$NTRODUCTION

Faced with another pile of laundry or muddy tracks across the living room rug, it is easy to lose track of your deeper purpose. *Sacred Motherhood* was written for mothers who seek to fulfill their soul's calling while simultaneously raising future generations—it offers women on the path of motherhood a guide back to themselves. In the throes of your everyday life, this book speaks to the eternal, sacred seed within you. It serves as a bridge between the profound soul-work that mothering entails and the tedious practicalities that incessantly tug at every mother's sleeve.

Before you became a mother, how did you describe your spiritual practice? Perhaps it was neatly defined as the time spent on your meditation cushion, moving through *asanas,* or communing with nature. Did you mourn the loss of this sacred time-out-of-time when mothering amped up to demand your full attention? Or perhaps you can still find ways to sneak off for a few moments of divine rapture before being called back to motherhood—the path of ultimate devotion.

Spiritual growth while on the ground and running is a telltale mark of motherhood. This book was written to help you embrace the reality that *this is your spiritual life*—every moment of every day, whether you are at the grocery store, changing diapers, arguing with your partner, snuggling with your baby, or dyeing your teenager's hair pink. This is the practice—the Sacred Motherhood practice. Bow to it. Pray for it. Greet the moments when you fall down as awakening opportunities, every bit as holy and powerful as the moments you can drop in and bliss out.

Spanning both the sacred and the mundane, *Sacred Motherhood* is written as a guide and journal, enticing you to pause momentarily to reflect and write, and then return to your mothering tasks armed with a heightened perspective, renewed vision, and creative ideas for enriching family life. For fifty-two weeks—a year of sacred motherhood—you are presented with thoughtful prompts and helpful reminders about the topic of the week as it relates to *you, your soul, and your child.*

Taking into consideration your limited time, and your need for beauty and companionship along the path of motherhood, *Sacred Motherhood* offers you weekly support through the seasons of motherhood. Brief passages meet you in your reality, inviting you to call in a new layer of intention and awareness in the midst of the everyday. This book was conceived by and for mamas dedicated to enhancing daily and yearly rhythms, and to cultivating mindful mothering while tending the inner flame of becoming.

Through affirmations and contemplations, *Sacred Motherhood* honors both the light and the shadow of motherhood. As you move through the seasons, open your arms to hold everything under the sun, because *everything is sacred, or nothing is sacred.* Chaos is sacred. Deep breaths are sacred. Tears are sacred. Childhood is sacred. Anything you cast into the shadows is likely to come back and haunt you. Wholeness, balance, and love—this is the way of *Sacred Motherhood.*

As we circle around the sun, each chapter calls up the unique energies and reflections that the current season evokes. If you are following along week by week, it will take you about three months to work your way through thirteen chapters, or one season. Around here, spring arrives sometime in March, which is an ideal time for new beginnings—and Week 1 of *Sacred Motherhood.* But perhaps you were inspired to buy the book at your bookstore as autumn's shorter days called you into a time of reflection, so you might want to dive in at Week 27. All is well—this is your book and your path. OWN IT! Pick up *Sacred Motherhood* whenever you feel called to it, and open it to whatever chapter speaks to you in the moment. This path is not about perfection; it's about following threads of inspiration, awareness, and joy through your days as a mother.

As you find your way through this book, don't try to do everything. Read each chapter with a tone of encouragement rather than expectation. Try the "Sacred Motherhood Practices" for a week, to see how they serve you on your path. Be open to new "Ideas" offered within each chapter, and have fun giving them a whirl. And dip into the suggested "Pairings." Pull out whatever makes you come more fully alive, leaving the rest for another day (or another lifetime). Trust that you are being guided to light on exactly what is called for in the present moment. We're all about *right timing!*

Sacred Motherhood, in fact, is the love child of synchronicity and right timing. The synchronicity landed when our previous books, Anni's *Sacred Pregnancy* and Niki's *The Mother's Wisdom Deck* (coauthored with Elizabeth Marglin), shared the same publication date—Mother's Day 2012. From then on, unlikely coincidences and twists of fate continued to weave our paths together until *Sacred Motherhood* eventually appeared on the horizon. The timing was perfect.

Anni was deeply involved in the creation of the Sacred Living Movement, traveling the world trying to bring women together in retreat to heal, open, share, and expand—all while being mother to four gorgeous, spiritual children. *Sacred Motherhood* had been gestating since Anni recognized the need to step beyond *Sacred Pregnancy* and embrace the next offering. This book dovetailed into her practice of trusting the rhythm of divine timing, and truly believing that everything we do as mothers in this lifetime ultimately is about our love for our children.

The glow of motherhood is all about trust and flow, and comes from the inner knowledge that our children chose us and have soul contracts to be with us on this journey. Anni knows that her four children guide her along her sacred path everyday, and that every moment the universe is happily colliding with perfection to bring her exactly where she needs to be. That is how she ended up here.

At the same time, Niki was just reframing her life to welcome a third child. Just as her older children turned toward independence and her life was about to reorient toward other passions, this unexpected blessing drew Niki back into the magical years of early childhood, when the path of motherhood is all-consuming. As she was opening to the mystery of life that keeps us on our soul's path, North Atlantic Books called to inquire about *Sacred Motherhood.*

Niki knew that a divine conspiracy was at play, and that her new baby girl, Story, was in on it. This book was conceived with Story in her womb, and written as Story slept and nursed next to her mama's heart. As "creative director," she has been present for every moment, guiding and inspiring Niki's contribution on behalf of a mystical new generation.

Initially, *Sacred Motherhood* was plotted and written as a long-distance conversation between two soul sisters who share a language of beauty, vision, color, and words. Much of the project's direction was more felt than spoken, and many pieces fell into place with ease. The book's creation was an extreme exercise in trusting the blessed flow and not freaking out as deadlines approached just as a baby was beginning to crawl, a family was moving cross-country, and both mamas were many winks shy of a good night's sleep. With only a few weeks to go before the deadline, Anni landed in her new home just down the road from Niki in Boulder, Colorado. It was as if the stars had fully aligned to make way for the birth of *Sacred Motherhood* with a final, miraculous push.

So here it is. In offering this creation to you, we've gathered a mother lode of material while raising our own children—seven children between our two families, ranging in age from one to seventeen. Yet we'd be the first to admit that we are not experts, nor is this book exhaustive. Rather, it is a living document of how we've struggled and where we've thrived while doing the dance of motherhood.

We are not perfect! We are no strangers to messy houses or crazed moments. We would not have been so dedicated to manifesting this book if we weren't in dire need of it ourselves. It is our gift to you— but we hope you'll accept that it is a WE gift. *Sacred Motherhood* was written as much to urge us along the winding path of mindful mothering as it was to inspire you.

In the end, we do hope our words, ideas, and images seed your path with beauty and understanding, reminding you that you already carry all the wisdom and grace it takes to mother in a sacred manner. No doubt you could add many tasty morsels that we have overlooked, or have yet to discover. We invite you to use the "Journal" section at the end of each chapter to record your own process and insights in what we hope may one day be a dog-eared and love-tattered testament of your mothering days.

Indeed, the sacred path of motherhood is all about the journey. And we're happy to have you walking alongside us, making it more beautiful and *epic* than we ever could if we were forging this path alone. We've found our tribe. Welcome, Sister!

If you feel sisterhood is part of your calling, we invite you to find a Sacred Motherhood Circle in your community, where you can bask in the support of women on this shared journey. Or attend a Sacred Motherhood Retreat, and learn how to gather and lead a circle of mothers dedicated to collectively honoring the path and practice of motherhood. And, check out all of the other Sacred Living Movement retreats and classes that can inspire your living and loving in this sacred Beauty Way.

Sun

Birth

New Beginnings

Chaos

Seeds

Adventure

Spirit

Blossoms

Babies

Creativity

Enlightenment

Inspiration

Rosebuds

Vision

Unconditional Love

Transformation

Faith

Joy

Oneness

The Call

sacred motherhood

Motherhood is a journey, and every journey begins with a call. In picking up this book, not only have you heard the call of motherhood, you have answered the call to Sacred Motherhood. Over the coming weeks, this book will serve as a guide, as you venture forth to claim the full truth and radiance of who you are on this path. There is no telling what you will discover along the way, but today you are saying YES *to this mysterious adventure by taking the first step.*

YOU ♻

What is the call? It works like this: For a while you are contented and fulfilled in your life. It may not be perfect, but you are happy even with the imperfections. Then one morning you wake up, and something is stirring within you. Your soul has been roused by a call that coaxes you out of your comfortable eddy and back into the river of life. The call may be faint or roaring, alluring or unwanted, strangely familiar or disturbingly unknown. Perhaps you feel compelled to respond and move toward whatever awaits. Perhaps you choose to ignore the invitation. In the end, it does not go away but only grows more pronounced, until it's as if your soul has grabbed you by the hair and is tugging you forward.

So here you are: You are a mother. Take a moment to remember how you were called to the journey of motherhood. Was the call unexpected, or long-awaited? What is now stirring within and calling you to walk the path of Sacred Motherhood? What fabulous forces delivered this book into your hands? What essential part of you is asking to be transformed or awakened? Are you willing? Are you ready?

YOUR SOUL ♻

Ready or not, motherhood is your calling. Your life has called you to the peak moments of motherhood as well as the trying ones, the boring ones, and the crazy-making ones. You have been called to serve and to play, to love and to grieve, to teach and to fail. You have been called to raise your highest self alongside your precious children. Not only is motherhood your calling, it is also your spiritual practice. This is it, and it's *sacred!*

While you may find a choice moment to sneak off and meditate or pray or prostrate yourself, every moment holds potential for your spiritual growth and awakening. Whether you are trawling the aisles of the grocery store, patching up your child's skinned knee, or spilling your coffee on a harried drive to work, every moment is sacred. How can you stay present and recognize this *truth* in the trenches of family life? How can you tend your own deep soul-work? This book meets you on the relentless and rewarding path of motherhood, adding weights to pull you into the heart of sacred living.

YOUR CHILD ☙

As you journey onward, it is essential that your children come along for the ride. Your babies have chosen you, Mama. And you have chosen them. It's a conspiracy. You were called into this life together for a reason; your souls are entwined. Rejoice in the gifts your children bring—and learn to welcome the challenges too, for they will serve as great teachers.

As a mother, remember that your children signed up for this journey with you as a package, complete with quirks, wounds, faults, and the mother lode of LOVE. You do not have to be perfect, so you can cross that off your list. Children come equipped with courage, forgiveness, guardian angels, and karma of their own. It is a wild ride, to be sure. Enjoy!

REFLECTIONS ☙

Motherhood—the shortest and steepest path to enlightenment.
ERIN ROSS, INTREPID MOTHER

This spunky quote says it all. It acknowledges the blood, sweat, and tears intensity of motherhood, but doesn't leaving you thinking that it is all for naught. Instead, it celebrates the rewards of committing to motherhood as a sacred path. Where have you glimpsed light, truth, and awakening amidst the daily ordeals and delights that define the mothering years?

SACRED MOTHERHOOD PRACTICE ☙

SET YOUR INTENTION. You've heard the call. Now say YES by setting an intention for this year of Sacred Motherhood. What essential qualities are you ready to claim for yourself and your family—beauty, forgiveness, joy? Who is that wise, empowered mother within who is ready to emerge? Write your intention as an "I AM" statement: "I am a sacred woman who walks a path of beauty with her children and manifests abundance for her people." Don't hold back. You are on this path— claim it!

IDEAS ☙

- MAKE A MOTHERHOOD MALA. A mala is a string of 108 prayer beads used by Hindus and Buddhists as they repeat a *mantra* (meditative word or phrase) or the name of a deity. Fashion a gorgeous one for yourself, as a commitment to approach motherhood as a spiritual practice. Pair your mala with a mantra, a prayer, or an affirmation that keeps you on the path—for instance, "Ma" (the mantra of the Great Mother), or "I am LOVE," or simply "Deep breath, deep breath, deep breath…."

- WATER YOUR SOUL. Integrate the sacred into basic elements of your day—start with your water. Place a crystal in your drinking glass to infuse the water you drink throughout the day with sacred vibrations. Use rose quartz for unconditional love, chrysoprase for healing, citrine for creativity, and so on. Follow any crystal "Pairings" suggestions for using these stones as you move through the year with *Sacred Motherhood.* And feel free to add some good vibes to your child's water as well. You can let the stone infuse the water for ten minutes, and then remove it before offering it to your child to avoid any danger of choking.

pairings ❧

- Book: *The Mother's Wisdom Deck* by Niki Dewart and Elizabeth Marglin, with illustrations by Jenny Kostecki-Shaw
- Music: "May I Suggest" by Red Molly and "The Way is Simple" by Hanna Leigh
- Sacred Living Movement Retreats: Sacred Motherhood

journal on

The Call

What called you to Sacred Motherhood? What new pathway is opening for you? What are you ready to
claim? Write your intention for this
year of Sacred Motherhood.

Birth

a mother is born

Spring is a time of birth and rebirth. Whether the recent birth of your child is still fresh in the air or the passing of time has seasoned this vital experience, this week we invite you to revisit your birth stories. Therein lie the remembrances of how your children came into the world, as well as the pregnant moment in which your life changed forever as you picked up the mantle of motherhood.

YOU ⌒

With the birth of her children, a woman crosses a threshold from one state of being to another. Celebrated as one of life's major passages, the transition from maiden to mother is permanent and binding. Once you are a mother, you will always be a mother.

Embracing this change is not always easy. Motherhood asks that you say goodbye to your old life, in order to step beautifully and confidently into a new manifestation of who you are. In traditions around the world, women are supported in moving from maidenhood to motherhood through rites of passage. These rituals appreciate what is being left behind, acknowledge the chaos and confusion of stepping across a threshold, and celebrate the mother who emerges on the other side.

You and your soul-sisters can honor this transformation for one another through a potent Blessing Way ceremony (originally inspired by Navajo healing rituals), held just before the birth journey begins. Through prayers and tears, such rituals open an energetic doorway to help the mama surrender to the mysteries of birth. (For more information and resources, check out the "Pairings" below.)

YOUR SOUL ⌒

Even without a special ceremony, birth serves as a rite of passage when marked and remembered through story. In giving birth, you enter a time-out-of-time in which you leave behind your usual way of being. With grace and grit, you journey to a place you never could have imagined. When you return and welcome your child, you are no longer the same person. Other channels to receiving a child into your life, such as adoption and surrogacy, are likewise songlines, or sacred pathways, to the creation of a mother.

In the journal entry below, you are prompted to write the unique story of your own birth into motherhood. Once it is written, share your story with your mother, sister, partner, or friend. The rite of recording and telling your story helps you bring the birth process to completion, and claim your place in the sacred circle of mothers.

YOUR CHILD ☙

For your child, birth is a monumental passage into this cycle of life. It is the major milestone in a child's separation from the spirit realm and the mother's womb. After birth, a baby is in a magical, transitional state. You can look into a newborn's eyes and experience pure, divine being. This is a time to stay in your protective nest, bonding and gathering strength. This stage of the birth process will eventually come to a close as the child is brought out into the larger world and welcomed into the community.

Each stage of birth serves the full integration of the child into Earthly existence, and can be ritualized, with ceremonies for cord-cutting, bathing, naming, and baby-blessing (see "Pairings" below). If your child is older and you feel that some piece of the birth journey is unfinished, you can also create rebirth opportunities. For example, my first child was born by cesarean delivery, and we have both carried trauma from this. By working with therapists and healers, and performing rituals to seal and release the experience, however, we've come a long way in honoring and amending our birth story.

REFLECTIONS ☙

The most important thing to remember this week is that every birth is unique and unfolds exactly as it is meant to be. Often we have expectations about the "ideal" birth, and may have work to do in order to come to peace with the reality of our actual birth experience.

Be gentle with yourself as you take this opportunity to reflect on your birth story and how it has shaped you and your children. Was it all you wanted it to be? Did your child come into the world in the peaceful, blissful way you had hoped? If you think you are holding onto birth pains and trauma, consider working with a trusted therapist who can help you process your story, or find a Sacred Living Movement Mother Roaster—a postpartum doula who uses traditional warming techniques to help new mamas heal—who can do a "sealing" ceremony in which you ritually close off the birth journey and cross the threshold into motherhood in a way that honors you and your journey. (Check our website for resources in your area: www .sacredpostpartum.net.)

SACRED MOTHERHOOD PRACTICE ☙

WRITE YOUR BIRTH STORIES. Record the story of each child's birth on beautiful paper and in a sacred manner. Even if you have done this before, take time to revisit the stories and see how they have evolved in your memory. With time, salient images emerge and new insights surface. Wrap up your writing and present it to your child at some important milestone: the first lost tooth, the thirteenth birthday, or at menarche (when menstruation begins).

IDEAS ☙

- TAKE A CEREMONIAL BATH. Mark the end of the birth process by ritually bathing with your child. Just as the waters of your womb sustained the life of your baby in utero, allow water to envelop and support both of you now as separate mother and child. Add your choice of salts and dried flowers to help heal old wounds and encourage the blossoming of new life stages.

- HONOR YOUR JOURNEY WITH A SELF-LOVE OIL AND CHANT. After birth, your body changes, and needs support to integrate the transformation. The loving Rose Oil recipe here was created for the Sacred Postpartum program, and can be a welcome help in healing and honoring your journey of motherhood at any time. Massage the oil onto your belly in the area of your womb in a clockwise, circular motion, and say:

I am healing

I am beautiful

I am thankful for all my body has to offer

My body is strong

My body continues to provide for my child.

ROSE OIL

1 cup of organic (pesticide-free) dried rose petals

organic virgin olive oil

pint or quart mason jar

Place the rose petals in the jar, and then fill the jar with organic virgin olive oil.

Slow Infusion: Allow the sun to warm the jar. Then place it in a dark place and let it sit for 3–4 weeks.

Fast Infusion: Set the jar of petals and oil into a pan with several inches of water, and warm over medium-low heat for 1–2 hours.

After the infusion is complete, strain the roses and store the Rose Oil in a glass jar.

· LEARN ABOUT HOW YOU CAME INTO THE WORLD. Sit down with your mom, dad, or another close relative, and let them spin the story of your beginning. Reflect on how your birth mirrors other aspects of your journey in this life.

pairings ෴

· Book: *Mother Rising: The Blessingway Journey into Motherhood* by Yana Cortlund, Barb Lucke, and Donna Miller Watelet

- Book: *Welcoming Ways: Creating Your Baby's Welcome Ceremony with the Wisdom of World Traditions* by Andrea Alban Gosline
- Sacred Living Movement Class: Sacred Baby Blessing (online)

Birth

Write the story of your birth
into motherhood: How have
you changed? What have you left
behind? What new gifts have you
claimed and incorporated into who
you are? How can you best share the
fullness of who you have become with your family and community?

Mindful Mothering

cultivating presence

*On the journey of motherhood, one of the most important lessons is how to be
present with yourself, your life, and your children. As your children push the limits
of your patience and understanding, they can lead you into places and situations
that you may find hard to accept. Nature, on the other hand, is a perfect reflection of presence. The harmony cultivated among everything living and breathing
in nature is divinity made manifest, and can teach us how to just BE with whatever just IS.*

YOU ❧

What is MINDFUL MOTHERING? It is the place where chaos collides
with your higher self, the place where you stand in your best moments
as a mother because you are fully *present and responsive* rather than simply
reactive. You are not attached to the outcome, but revel in your ability to just BE. This is the you to strive for—the you that spiritual practice helps cultivate.

We all have the capacity to live in this conscious awareness. When
we do, we are the best mothers we can be with the knowledge we
hold at this moment in time. Mindful mothering invites us to live
in Divine Mind, which means that we respond with love rather than
reacting with prerecorded tapes from past junk that may not serve
anyone, much less the current situation. When we are acting from
love and staying in the present moment, we are not bothered by the
two-year-old's temper tantrum or the mess in the kitchen, or kids
crying because something isn't fair.

Learning to mother with mindfulness means that you respond
with love, as much as you are able. It means being present and
patient with both yourself and your children. And it means growing
into the mother that you want to be, by staying open to discovering
who that is and how she shows up for her children.

YOUR SOUL ❧

If you want to bring mindful mothering into your daily practice, you
can start by practicing Zen Beginner Mind, which always and in all

ways starts with *gratitude*. When you feel true gratitude for simply being alive, you are able to open up to this innocent state of being.

Zen Beginner Mind keeps you fresh, like a newborn baby who is pure and willing to learn. In this state you are also curious, like a trusting child who asks for teachings. Whether they come from your children, your elders, your mistakes, or your triumphs, these teachings can shape how you mother, how you create, and how you dance through the flow of your life.

YOUR CHILD ☙

Children know when we are being reactive as opposed to responsive; they know when we are loving rather than angry; and they can tell when we practice mothering in awareness—because they can read us like a simple children's board book. We teach best by example, so when we *practice* mindfulness, our children can learn how to listen to themselves, quiet their minds, and follow their hearts in loving response. Isn't this what we hope for our children? The more they see us practice mindfulness and gratitude, the more they will imitate those practices and actions, and they will begin to understand from very early on that they have a "go-to place" within themselves that can answer life's questions with clarity.

REFLECTIONS ☙

When something gets shaken up in your home, do you find that you are quick to react rather than to respond in love? Are you less present and less conscious than you would like to be with yourself and your family? If you answered YES, you are not alone! Join the sacred sisterhood and begin a daily mindfulness practice that will stir more gratitude, learning, and awareness within you.

SACRED MOTHERHOOD PRACTICE ☙

BEGIN EACH DAY WITH GRATITUDE. Every morning when you wake up, immediately name three things for which you are grateful. Do this practice for thirty days, and see how it goes; see how inviting gratitude into your day begins to change your life. After the first thirty days, take up the practice for another sixty days, and so forth.

ÎDEAS ᐤᐤ

· CREATE A GRATITUDE JOURNAL. Find a beautiful blank book, and make it a journal of your Sacred Motherhood year. Use it for jotting down your daily gratitudes, as treasured little reminders and touchstones for hard times. Keep the journal by your bed, where you can add to it each morning, and revisit it in the evening to carry gratefulness into your dreamtime.

· PRACTICE ZEN BEGINNER MIND. Find something you always wanted to learn to do but never did. It should be something you know nothing about and would like to challenge yourself to undertake. Now, stand up, put your hands on your heart, and close your eyes. Listen to all of the sounds around you. Hold a feeling of gratitude, and then open to Zen Beginner Mind. In this state, ask for guidance about what you need to do to pursue this new path. Do not judge the answers; just let them BE.

PAÎRÎNGS ᐤᐤ

· Book: *Everyday Blessings: The Inner Work of Mindful Parenting* by Myla and Jon Kabat-Zinn
· Children's book: *The Three Questions* by John J. Muth
· Music: "Mahalo" by Mary Isis

journal on
Mindful Mothering

Use the space here to create a new daily mindful-mothering practice. What could you dedicate yourself to doing that would bring more conscious awareness to your everyday family life? And how can you make that happen?

Mother Love

expanding your heart

It's spring, and love is in the air. Then again, for a mama, love is always in the air! It is the crown jewel of motherhood. Mother love knows no bounds, and banishes all other conditions. As a channel of this divine elixir, your focus this week is on the heart.

YOU ❦

When a child comes into your life, your heart enlarges to unprecedented proportions. Even when it feels full to bursting with your first child, it miraculously expands to hold infinitely more love as other children arrive. A love so large is truly divine—but it can also be scary and overwhelming. Most poignantly, the dread, fear, or tragic reality of losing a child is almost unbearable. Your wide-open, deeply invested heart is tender, and therein lies its strength. Find the courage to live the *enormity* of your love!

Fortunately, your heart is exquisitely designed to love and care for each child as an extension—or better yet, an evolution—of yourself. But as love blurs the edge where you leave off and your children begin, take care that you do not unintentionally project your ideals onto them, which can thwart the free flow of your love. Your buried hopes or expectations about how your children should look or behave can prevent you from loving them just as they are. As they grow, their uniqueness may delight and repel you in turns. And in the teenage years, all may seem lost!

YOUR SOUL ❦

Do not despair. Underneath all your human foibles, you love all your children *no matter what.* In this way, children are love gurus: They teach us to love even when it hurts. They teach us to love when we disagree. They teach us to love on faith. They teach us to love each inimitable being for all the gifts and challenges he or she brings into this life.

Your children are indeed keys to unlock the divine energy of love that dwells within you and all of us. Children are not the source of this love, although they carry it in spades. Rather, when you are in their presence, the floodgates open for you to experience the love that you are. When you *own this love*, you can live it. You can be "in love" with everyone and everything.

YOUR CHILD ⌐∿

If ever you feel a loss of love, remember that with children in your life you have a steady current of love at your fingertips. Nestle up with your little love-beings. Hold them every chance you get, heart-to-heart. In this space, trust your heart when it proclaims that love is the most powerful energy in the universe.

The love a mother shares with her children is exceptional not only in quantity but also in quality. Identified and named by the Greeks, *agape* is the selfless kind of love that gods or parents have for their children; it is unconditional, and given with or without reciprocation. Similarly, *karuna* is a Tantric term describing the compassionate love of the goddess, or of a mother for her child, that embodies loving-kindness, trust, tenderness, and touch, thus laying the foundation for healthy relationships and intimacy throughout life. Revel in the experience as you fall into this sacred love-lineage!

REFLECTIONS ⌐∿

Love is contagious. As you let your love shine, those around you may feel love stir within them, and remember that they too are love. For everyone's sake, make a vow to feed the love within you.

What makes you feel love? An intimate moment with your partner? A sweet snuggle with your baby? A swim in the ocean? Do whatever it takes to make your love *grow and overflow*.

SACRED MOTHERHOOD PRACTICE ⌐∿

OFFER EACH FAMILY MEMBER A DAILY EXPRESSION OF YOUR LOVE. Be creative, consistent, and considerate of each individual's love language (check out the "Pairings" section below). This practice feels yummy to everyone on the receiving end, and fans the flames of love within you too.

IDEAS ❦

- SAY IT WITH LOVE. Although everyone loves to hear the tried and true "I love you," have fun expanding your repertoire to include other terms of endearment. You can't go wrong with heartfelt appreciation ("Thank you for being in my life!") or sincere praise ("This picture makes my heart happy because it reminds me of spring!"). You might also try expressing the joy you feel thanks to your child ("I love watching you play soccer!"). As you experiment, remember that your heart carries the crucial ingredient—feel the love before you say it.

- ADD LOVE TO YOUR JOURNAL. With some special paper and your loving hands, shower your Sacred Motherhood journal with love. Then use it as a place to commemorate love, along with your gratitude (see Week 3). Write down all the little and big things that speak of love each day—the way the sun shines on everyone, the feel of your little one's hand in yours, or the poem that reminds you of your mother.

PAIRINGS ❦

- Book: *The Five Love Languages of Children* by Gary Chapman and Ross Campbell

- Crystal: Rose quartz is the stone of love and peace. It opens the heart chakra to promote unconditional love, compassion, forgiveness, and harmony.

Mother Love

Take a walk through your past, and recall all the ways in which you have experienced love. Who has loved you? How do you know? How have you expressed love to those who captured your heart? Moving forward, how do you want to love? And how do you want to be loved?

_____

_____

_____

_____

_____

_____

_____

_____

_____

_____

_____

_____

_____

Sacred Feminine

the goddess within

This week, Sacred Motherhood gets juicy. Amrita—the Sanskrit word for the nectar of the gods—is flowing, inviting you to savor the divinity within you. Though you are not immortal, you may tap the infinite well of the sacred feminine through the lineage of the Great Mother that you serve here on Earth.

YOU ℮〜

On days when you become mired in the mundane details of motherhood, it is easy to forget that you carry a piece of the Mother Goddess within you. This life-giving superpower elevates the path of motherhood with a dusting of divinity. Like all divine mothers across time and traditions, you are a *creatrix*—you channel creativity and life through your very being.

Are you in touch with your sacred feminine vibe? Many mamas are not. From disappointing birth stories to lackluster libido, motherhood can make many women feel anything but goddess-like. And no wonder! Thousands of years ago, the patriarchy took center stage, and the divine feminine went underground. Women lost sight of the sacred source of their power. They forgot that, as daughters of the Goddess, a divine feminine energy vibrates through their veins, breasts, and wombs.

It's time for the Goddess to come out of hiding, so that all women can remember how to love their bodies, birth their babies, and take pleasure in life. In resurrecting the gifts of the divine feminine, mothering can also be celebrated as *sacred* work once again.

YOUR SOUL ℮〜

Just as some goddesses have more maternal energy than others, not all women choose the path of motherhood. But you have been called to be a source and sustainer of life, and through mothering you can awaken the beauty and power of the divine feminine. This abundant, primal life-force is ever-present in the universe, and available to you at any moment. It is not something that you have to pursue, achieve, or manifest. Instead, sacred feminine power flows through you when you simply soften.

Fortunately, motherhood teaches us how to soften—your body softens to bring forth new life, your breasts soften to suckle your babes, your lap softens to receive a child in need, and your agendas soften so that you may be of service. In softening, you open to the deliciousness of loving and living. Your inner goddess stirs, and you open to receive the creativity, vitality, and juiciness of the Great Mother.

YOUR CHILD ⌒〜

As the blessings of the divine feminine rain down upon you, how might you "pay it forward" to your children? What does it mean to mother as a vessel of the Goddess? You're sacred, right? So too are your children. Their antics are sacred. Their tantrums are sacred. Their dirty socks are sacred. Everything is sacred, or nothing is sacred. There is no need to judge or resist. Keep your channels open to the joy and love that surrounds your family.

As you raise your children, in however sacred a manner, you will still fall upon despairing and desperate times that will bring you to your knees. When you reach those low points, lie down in the lap of the Goddess, and in her embrace return to grace. Divine grace is there to catch your children when they stumble as well, for they too are children of the Great Mother. The more you can surrender your fear and resistance, the more you can relax into knowing that you are not alone.

REFLECTIONS ⌒〜

Motherhood offers plenty of tense moments when you most need to summon the Goddess. But in tensing, you cut yourself off from this power. During the intensity of labor, vocalizing can clear the way for the miracle of birth. Similarly, I find mantras to be one of the fastest ways to open channels for the life-giving energy of the divine feminine. Alone in the kitchen or at a *kirtan* (sacred chanting) event, try unleashing your voice to create resonance throughout your body and expand the field of your heart.

SACRED MOTHERHOOD PRACTICE ⌒

CREATE AN ALTAR TO THE GODDESS WITHIN YOU. Begin by finding a space in your home that you can claim for the sacred feminine. Whether it's a tiny nook or a whole room, wrap it in beauty worthy of a goddess. Now meditate on your inner goddess. What does she like? What is her color? How do you court her into revealing her full radiance—with flowers? Candles? Crystals? Or maybe bones?

IDEAS ⌒

- FIND YOUR INNER GODDESS. From the ample ranks of the divine feminine, a goddess is alive and well within you. Do your research. Who is she—Quan Yin, Pachamama, Mary, Demeter, Kali? Get her gear, and get your goddess on. And don't forget to place her image in a position of honor upon your altar.

- RAISE YOUR SHAKTI. When you are on the verge of collapse, call upon Shakti, the Goddess of divine feminine energy and creative power. She's got your back, literally—summon her energy up from the base of your spine by breathing, undulating your hips, and opening your root chakra. Visualize Shakti as your own sacred feminine power, building and rising up through your chakras to the top of your head.

PAIRINGS ⌒

- Book: *Awakening Shakti: The Transformative Power of the Goddesses of Yoga* by Sally Kempton

- Class (not Sacred Living Movement): Redmoon Mystery School: Following Shamanic Pathways to the Divine Feminine with Nikiah Seeds (www.redmoonmysteryschool.com)

- Crystal: Moonstone is said to be made from the tears of a moon goddess, and carries potent divine feminine power that can activate the *kundalini shakti* (feminine energy) coiled at the base of spine. It is also a stone of mystery and revelation, and can help in understanding and assimilating all aspects of oneself.

With words, paints, and/or collage, use this space to describe and express your inner goddess.

Creativity

rousing inspiration

Mother Nature is a supreme creatrix. She creates without critique or bias, and she paints the colors of the Earth and sky with infinite imagination and free-dom—because she can. While the landscape changes from season to season, her Beauty-Way touch remains as constant as the rising and setting sun. This week, as you rouse your creativity, looking to the sacred feminine for inspiration can be the perfect place to start. And you won't have to look far!

YOU ☙

Becoming a mother is the ultimate act of creation. After all, you co-created and gave birth to a HUMAN! Talk about a Nature Goddess—wow! And for you mamas who have manifested your families in a different, equally sacred manner, your power of intention is clearly some potent, creative juju. Let's just pause for a moment, in serious wonderment. Now that we have established that you are in cahoots with the divine, there is truly nothing you can't create, right?

Life is meant for more than a daily grind. Birthing your ideas and growing them into what they are meant to be is a way to share your own flavor of sweet nectar with the world. If you deny your creative soul's calling, you will always have a feeling of longing. If you don't go for your dreams, you will always wonder. One thing I can tell you is that there is *never* a perfect time to go for *anything.* Life is just a series of cliffs that you jump off—ready or not!

YOUR SOUL ☙

Creativity is the food of the soul. It speaks in every language, and manifests in every color, shape, and size. Creativity is truly a force to be reckoned with. I know that when I get the inspiration to create something, I am so moved by my passion that I have no choice but to dive in immediately. When my muse kicks in, I feel unstoppable. As women, as mothers, we are capable of anything!

The beautiful thing about embracing your creative inspiration is that there is only one you, which means that everything you create will indeed be your "original" soul creation. When you make something from nothing, you bring the divine energy that lives through you into real form in the physical realm. Creating your unique vision is your sacred signature on the world!

YOUR CHILD ☙

Children are born creative, and the only thing that stops them from unfolding that innate gift is interference from various outside influences. Children are built to learn through imitation. When we allow very little children access to media, for example, they do not have a chance to tap their creative play as deeply or as often as they would otherwise. Media is designed to think for them, thus informing their play and creations. So, if children are imitating what they are watching on the screen, they are pulling from their media influence rather than their own creative and spiritual library.

It's so important for you to take the creative lead in your home! Your children learn from you how to dive into their own passions, live unafraid of their creative ideas, and follow the crazy, silly inspirations that could quite possibly turn into incredible masterpieces. If you cultivate a creative home environment filled with inviting, open-ended media like quality paints, pencils, paper, clay, yarn, silk cloths, sticks, shells, and stones, and allow them to explore in the outdoors, your children will have all they need to dive into the imaginative miracle of childhood.

REFLECTIONS ☙

When you have an idea, what do you do with it? Do you massage it, love it, and put it out into the world? Or do you say to yourself, "Nobody will like it," or—how about this doozy?—"I will get to that someday"? If so, remember that life is much richer with *your* creative seeds sprinkled all over it! Envision yourself making a wish on a dandelion puff, and seeing all those dandy little softies floating away and landing all over the world, just like your creations. Make your ideas do MORE OF THAT! Close your eyes, say YES to your creativity, and let your inspiration take wing!

SACRED PREGNANCY PRACTICE ⁓

ROUSE YOUR INSPIRATION. Whether it's painting, drawing, collaging, knitting, cooking, dancing, or whatever, open that creative space within you, every single day. Take one step toward turning your inspiration into *something,* and share it with your children, your friends, and the whole wide world.

IDEAS ⁓

- MAKE A SACRED ART BOOK. Create a special space to dash off poetic thoughts, paint inspired images, develop your zany ideas, or scribble like a child. Buy a blank sketchbook, and make a collage of images, words, and color on the cover to make it your go-to place for creative play. Invite your children to make one too!

- REMIND YOURSELF TO BE CREATIVE. Write this mantra out and place it on your mirror: *"Creativity is food for my soul!"*

PAIRINGS ⁓

- Book: *The Creative Family* by Amanda Blake Soule
- Crystal: Wear a citrine necklace to attract abundance and creativity. You can also throw a citrine stone in your drinking water to help activate your creative soul—as long as you are drinking with awareness and intention!
- Sacred Living Movement Retreat: Sacred Art (online)
- Music: "She Is Boundless" by Mary Isis

Draw here. Collage here. Write some poetry here about what it means to be a bad-ass, creative goddess of a mother! Let your ideas unfold first here, and then expand on them in the art journal you are creating. Don't hold back. Unleash your creative Wild Woman!

Inner Flame

*keeping your
passions alive*

This week, we look deeply at your passions, and help you find the spark that lives within your heart center. Being a mother is ALL passion, because it's the deep-est heart-work you'll ever do. Yet there is even more to the depths of who you are as a woman. In the spring, your dreams are fresh and full of life. Let's find ways to grow them into reality.

YOU ⟡

The passionate spark that breathes life into each of us is unique. When we tap into that spark, we can light up a room with our brilliant, glow-ing energy. Becoming a mother redefines who we are in the world, and sometimes that spark—which once may have been filled with poetry and passion—becomes less sparkly.

While I am deeply proud of my motherhood role, I am also proud of the work I do in the world, and the passions I have pursued. You too are the whole map of your life, and while the terrain of moth-erhood can be all-consuming at times, there are many roads that didn't dead-end when you became a mother, even if it may have felt that way.

Sometimes, to explore these roads, you need to blow your own mind! Do you know what I mean? Blowing your mind means explod-ing the boxes you live within, and allowing yourself to be filled with wonder and amazement at who you are in the world. It means you are willing to fire up your passions in a way that teaches your children about the infinite possibilities afforded to us as human beings.

Maybe your dreams have shifted since becoming a mother. What-ever the case, you don't have to wait to bring them to life. Your children can become a part of your vision, and can even provide more inspiration as you get going on living it out!

YOUR SOUL ⟡

Your *inner flame* is bold and without fear. It is the very definition of what is passionate and free—it's kinda bad-ass. It'll look you right in the eye and won't blink, because it can see past your hesitation and help you go deeper. It's the fun and flirty, sensual and playful side of you. It's the fire in your belly.

What if you were as *free and fearless* as your inner flame? Your inner flame is an adventure waiting to happen. It tells you it's okay to travel and sink into another culture, to follow your dreams, to be the bright and beautiful YOU that you were meant to be. It allows you to shine, and coaxes you out of the shadows to play in the spotlight. This is the soul-spark of your passions.

YOUR CHILD ☙

Children are born passionate about everything! They feel every emotion, and experience every situation, in extremes—whether playing, creating, dancing, or even eating. They do not know any other way to be, except to fully feel and express everything out loud. As our babies grow, they learn to temper those extremes and pull back. The trick is helping them to never lose the spark they had when they came into this life.

Teaching your child to listen to his heart is critical, because he has a destiny to fulfill—a destiny that belongs to him alone. In order to live that out, he must know how to tune out all the chatter and listen to the voice of his soul, so that he can find out what his passions truly are. Pay attention to your child's inner light; notice his interests, what seems to excite him and feed his soul fire. Encourage your child's exploration deep into these interests. Help him dive into the fullness of who he is meant to be in the world.

REFLECTIONS ☙

We all have an inner light that glows more brightly when we are living our deepest desires and following our heart's path. What stirs you to action? What really turns you on and moves you so deeply that you have no choice but to act on it immediately? Dig deep, and ask yourself how often you say YES to following your passions—and how often you stop yourself. Do you have any self-limiting beliefs that dim the inner light leading to your passions?

SACRED MOTHERHOOD PRACTICE ⌒

TEND YOUR INNER FLAME. This week, commit to doing one thing each day that fans your soul-fire. Read a poem while taking a potty break, add a new spice to your routine supper, or wear a red scarf. It doesn't matter what you do—what matters is that you stay lit up!

IDEAS ⌒

- CREATE A VISION BOARD. Get out the magazines, glue, glitter, and paints. Cut out or paint any images that reflect your dreams and passions. Now collage them onto a large poster board or canvas panel, and add embellishments until the whole creation lights your fire. Hang it where it can inspire you to grow your dreams and turn your vision into reality.

- FOLLOW THE PATH OF PASSION. Pay careful attention to whatever passions are stirring in your child. There may be some that you haven't noticed before, or some that look different from this new angle. Choose one, and support your child in manifesting this dream. Sign her up for a class, get a book out of the library for her, or invite her to draw brilliant pictures of her heart's desire.

PAIRINGS ⌒

- Crystal: Wear ruby or garnet, or place them at all four corners of your bed, to ignite more passion and amplify your energy.
- Music: "Whole Wide World" by Mindy Gledhill, and "Girl on Fire" by Alicia Keys

journal on

Inner Flame

Write about your inner flame, your passions, and your desires. What really turns you on, and moves you so deeply that you must act on it immediately? What kind of action would honor your spark?

Do it with JOY

claiming your bliss

In our household, we have a saying: "Do it with JOY!" We also hold that if you cannot connect with joy in doing something, DON'T DO IT! Take a break. Do something else. Shift your worldview. Most importantly, claim your bliss.

When you do anything in life—go to work, pay bills, change diapers, or drive the carpool—find the enjoyment, and infuse each act with love. This commitment to joy creates positive energy in your home and in your life. Though the concept is simple, mastery remains elusive for many. This week, take up the joy challenge!

YOU ☙

The motherhood doldrums have sapped us all at one time or another. Beyond the usual ebb and flow of good times and bad, sometimes a funk settles in, and every moment offers up more fuel for this foul mood. The kids are arguing, the milk has gone bad, and your partner has to work late. Meanwhile, the trees are budding, and a warm breeze softly rustles your toddler's curls. You are drowning in self-pity while floating in an ocean of delights.

How can you resuscitate your bliss? It's time for a joy revival. Turn on your choice of lively music, and get cooking. Whip up one of your favorite frivolous dinners (popcorn, anyone?) and eat it by candlelight. Let all of the "shoulds" fall away, and do whatever makes your heart happy. What you, the world, and your family need more than a spotless kitchen floor is your JOY.

YOUR SOUL ☙

If joy visits too seldom, or low spirits plague your home life, it may be time for radical reappraisal. Joy is your birthright; what is keeping you from your innate enjoyment? Have you worn away your vital reserves? Are you wrapped up in negatively judging yourself or others? Do you feel guilty if you are having too much fun? Are you unconsciously feeding misery and starving out happiness? These are ponderous questions that are best approached with care—and a hint of a smile, if possible.

There are times when depression feels ponderous and you need to seek professional support, of course. Otherwise, try tackling your killjoy dilemma by focusing on just one task that you do not enjoy. Let's say you hate to pick up the daily debris of toys, socks, and quinoa. As you begin this loathsome job, notice what is arising underneath your dislike—resentment? Boredom? Your inner critic? You may be surprised, even enlightened, by what you discover. With this newfound awareness, identify what could bring you back to joy— and DO IT!

YOUR CHILD ❧

Apply this same remedy to your children when they grumble. Ask your kids, "Are you doing that with joy? If not, how can you find your joy?" This will help ease them back to their natural pursuit of happiness. If they continue to struggle, take a step closer to see if perhaps you have saddled them with an unrealistic expectation. Or maybe they just need a snack.

Also remember that children learn by imitating the adults in their lives. When you encounter a habitual gripe ("Do I have to do my homework?"), consider whether they may have learned this from you; remember that the apple does not fall far from the tree. Be honest. How might you be creating a culture of complaint? If you do whatever you do with joy, they will follow your lead.

REFLECTIONS ❧

As you work hard and do well, do not forget to embrace life's simple pleasures. No matter how busy you feel, make time for a daily dose of delight. Wake early to enjoy the sunrise, or slowly savor an evening cup of tea. Leave silly notes in your kids' lunches, or tell jokes at the dinner table. Hug your honey when he or she comes home. Eat watermelon. What you nurture will grow—let joy be what you cultivate in motherhood.

SACRED MOTHERHOOD PRACTICE ࿊

JUST FOR THIS WEEK, DO EVERYTHING WITH JOY. Even if it feels forced, just give it a go. Ask your children to do this as well. And make "DO IT WITH JOY!" a new family mantra.

IDEAS ࿊

- PLAN A JOY REVIVAL. Sometimes it is hard to lift ourselves up when we are spiraling downward. Next time you are in a really good mood, plan ahead by writing down some of your favorite "joy-revival" activities on small slips of paper. Place these prompts in a "basket of joy." When you can't seem to shake a bad attitude, pull out one of your prompts, and let it lead you to a better day.
- MAKE AN UPLIFTING SPRITZER. Invite your children to join you in mixing up spritzers to keep at the ready should you ever need to dispel negativity and return to joy.

UPLIFTING SPRITZER

1 oz. distilled water

5–10 drops of an essential oil (or a pleasing blend of oils) known to arouse happiness such as: orange, bergamot, lemon, rose, jasmine, and ylang-ylang

Mix all ingredients in a one-ounce spray bottle, and spritz yourself as needed.

PAIRINGS ࿊

- Book: *Raising Happiness: 10 Simple Steps for More Joyful Kids and Happier Parents* by Christine Carter
- Music: "Put Your Records On" by Connie Bailey Rae, and "Glorious" by MaMuse

Do it with JOY

What do you do every day with joy? What do you do without joy? If you find you are doing more things without joy, how can you SWITCH IT UP?

Imperfection

no mud, no lotus

There are no problems, only opportunities! Every situation in life is a series of choices. Saying YES *to life, with all its ups and downs, is all about perception—and you get to choose how you perceive every single moment. The wild abandon of new life bursting forth everywhere in springtime teaches us that there is perfection in just* ALLOWING *things to happen. Even seeing the weeds with "beauty eyes" helps us to understand that the glitches and messes in our lives are perfect, when viewed through a different lens.*

YOU ❧

At any moment, you have a choice that either leads you closer to your spirit or further away from it.
—THICH NHAT HANH

Every situation is an opportunity to grow. If you take this approach to life, then applying judgments to any circumstance will not be necessary. Nothing is simply "bad," and nothing is "good." Everything "just is." Within that "just is" you will find important life lessons and valuable information about your destiny. Motherhood presents countless opportunities to find the beauty in the mess. Your response is what shapes your day—and ultimately your life.

YOUR SOUL ❧

As you step toward inspired living, it is far more important to keep your soul clean of energetic messes than to obsess over the physical messes in your life. Spilled milk and dirty hands can be cleaned up more easily than hurt feelings or wounded pride. In truth, these household messes are only problems because of your attachment to some other idea of how of things should be. If you can let go of "perfection" along with the illusion of being in control, then you are less likely to react negatively, and can experience living without judgment and fear. When you free your soul from judgment and fear, you can believe in miracles; you can be pure love; and you can live in joy, even within the royal mess of family life. The present moment is all you have. The beautiful lotus flower, a symbol of purity and enlightenment, rises through dirty water to bloom in the open air even though its roots are in mud. If you get mired in the mud, you will never grow the lotus.

YOUR CHILD ☙

All this is easier said than done, right? What about the day your child decides to color on your newly refinished table? Sometimes you have to muster every ounce of love and nonattachment in order to *respond* rather than react. When you react, you are not typically in your loving Divine Mind. When you choose to respond, on the other hand, you must first take a moment to release whatever layers of emotional scripts may be playing out in your mind. Let the anger and disappointment move through and out of you. As you feel your heart and mind opening again, you will be able to speak from your higher self and promote a healthier exchange.

In this example, there are several different pathways available to you: You can get angry, and react with upset because of your attachment to the table looking a certain way. Or you can choose to respond with a "fix-it" attitude, and say something like, "Tables are for holding things, not for coloring on. Let's find a way to clean the table together." Or, you can even say, "While we don't normally color on furniture, you have created a lovely piece of artwork," and then highlight the colored section as the "honored" spot at the table. Do you see how the same situation can generate such varied outcomes, based on your initial response?

What if your child throws a temper tantrum at the store? If you are attached to your child acting "perfectly," a meltdown could send you into a reactive mode and have you yelling at your child to behave. Instead, you could meet your child's need for extra love and understanding in that moment by dropping down to his eye level and wrapping him in your loving embrace.

Which pathway feels better to you? Reflect on how you tend to view messy situations, and how you might turn them into teachable moments for yourself and your child.

REFLECTIONS ❧

Take time to ponder your own childhood: How was perfection regarded in your home? Were the objects in your home more important than people's feelings? Were you expected to behave "perfectly," or were you given freedom to express your views and ideas with creative purpose? Can you see similarities in how you parent your own child?

SACRED MOTHERHOOD PRACTICE ❧

LET GO OF PERFECTION. This week, try developing a different relationship to the messes that surround you. Don't judge yourself if the kitchen is not clean. Encourage your child to jump in mud puddles. Set aside your knee-jerk reactions, and make more conscious choices about how you want to meet—or even embrace—the imperfection of motherhood.

IDEAS ❧

- PRACTICE NONATTACHMENT. Give away something of deep meaning to you, such as a favorite necklace or cherished piece of art. Offer it freely and with the intention of truly letting it go, to brighten someone else's day.

- TRY THE ART OF ZENTANGLE. Check out a book about Zentangles, a new approach to meditative drawing that turns simple lines and patterns into art. The trick is to stay present and nonattached. There are no mistakes or expectations, only beauty and fun to share with your little ones.

PAIRINGS ❧

- Books: *Joy of Zentangle* by Design Originals with contributing artists Suzanne McNeill, Sandy Steen Bartholomew, and Marie Browning, and *No Mud, No Lotus, The Art of Suffering* and *Peace is Every Step* by Thich Nhat Hanh

journal on

Imperfection

Write your thoughts about attachment, perfection, and the messes of motherhood. Note any changes you want to make. Allow yourself time and space to explore what "no mud, no lotus" means in your life.

Sacred YES
+ Holy NO

understanding boundaries

As the Earth warms, nature blossoms in flexibility with every supple bud, leaf, and flower bending toward the light and life to create spring's colorful tapestry. With nature as our mirror, this week we will look at how you too flex or stand firm to the tune of YES and NO.

YOU ᥫᨀ

A mother's work is medicine, and when you choose a life of service, whether to your family, your career, or your passions, you choose to be *worthy* of sharing your medicine. Make certain that is your truth. *Are you worthy?* Have you checked your ego at the door, and can you say YES to showing up in service, with a shining heart full of love? Sharing your heart medicine can also move you out of balance and integrity, if you give and give without setting boundaries. This is when "no" needs to become a Holy NO.

"Sacred YES and Holy NO" is a mantra that can help raise your awareness around the many choices you make each day. And it can support you in setting boundaries as you offer yourself in service to others. A Sacred YES is a "yes" that you give with your whole heart—but only after you have sat with the situation at hand and attempted to truly understand what is being asked of you. This means that when you say YES, you do so without strings attached, and with a free and loving heart.

A Holy NO is a "no" you use to set a sacred boundary that honors your heart-choice at that moment in time. You are saying NO with consciousness. It is deeply important to honor who you are and what you need.

YOUR SOUL ᥫᨀ

Protecting your soul from overspending its *prana* (life-force) is just as important as being able to give it away. As mothers, we give all day long, and the output can be exhausting if we don't set personal boundaries. Sometimes we habitually say "no" to simple requests made by our children, rather than allowing the flexibility and freedom of YES to rule the day. This often happens when we have neglected to use our Holy NO for boundary-setting, and have nothing left to give. The balancing act of YES and NO is about showing up for yourself and your children! When you bring awareness to how you give of yourself, you are able to focus your truest heart's desire and say Sacred YES and Holy NO with generosity and love.

YOUR CHILD ☙

Your children ask many things of you in a day: "Mom, watch my new trick!" "Mom, can I paint?" "Mom, can we cook spaghetti right now?" This happens over and over again throughout the day. Many times, as a normal mama, you may just be tired and shoot off a quick "not right now" because it's easier in the moment.

Take a deep look at how often you say the word "no" in a day (or some variation of it). If this feels out of balance for you, try rewriting your script to use NO consciously and sparingly. If you say "no" too much, your children may stop asking for those creative moments to unfold throughout the day—which could eventually limit what they think is possible in life. But remember to only say "yes" when you can make it a Sacred YES! And, don't be afraid to use a healthy Holy NO when it is called for in the name of safety, sanity, and/or serenity.

REFLECTIONS ☙

Do you find that you just say YES to everything that is asked of you? Or are you the type of person that is reluctant to give of yourself even when you can? Do not judge yourself harshly either way; just notice. This noticing is critical because, unless you know your proclivities, you cannot live in fully conscious awareness, nor can you make fully conscious decisions about your life. Do you think you are generally a NO person or a YES person?

SACRED MOTHERHOOD PRACTICE ☙

MAKE "SACRED YES AND HOLY NO" YOUR MANTRA. Using your motherhood mala (prayer beads) from Week I, focus your daily practice on repeating "Sacred YES and Holy NO" 108 times—one time for each bead on your mala. This will anchor the mantra in your being, allowing you to keep it in your consciousness throughout the day and helping you to manifest clear and honorable boundaries.

ÎDƐAS ℰ⁓

- SHARE YOUR MANTRA. Invite your children to use the "Sacred YES and Holy NO" mantra, and help them to understand what it means by bringing it to life through your daily interactions.

- CHANGE YOUR TUNE. Try surprising your kids by saying YES to something you typically respond to with a NO. It can be fun for everyone when mama flexes to welcome possibility and spontaneity.

pAÎRÎNƧS ℰ⁓

- Flower Essence: A Bach Flower Essence called "Centaury" supports boundary-setting, inner strength, and self-determination.

- Herbal Ally: Use motherwort to help you set loving boundaries as a mother. Brew up "Sacred YES and Holy NO" tea as needed (except during pregnancy).

SACRED YES + HOLY NO TEA

1 tsp. dried motherwort

1 tsp. dried mint (for taste)

Combine herbs and steep in 1 cup of boiling water for 10 minutes. Do not use during pregnancy.

journal on

Sacred YES
+ Holy NO

Write about times you remember using a Sacred YES and /or a Holy NO. Now turn to the present moment. Is there anything you need to say YES to, in order to open up new possibilities? Are there any boundaries that you need to set, using the Holy NO in support of living your truth?

Wild Motherhood

letting your hair down

As flowers pop out wild and reborn this time of year, they are free to move and twist and get entangled in every new moment under the springtime sun. The wind may carry their petals to far-off adventures, or they may continue to grow radiant and colorful where they have blossomed. But the one constant is that they drink deeply from the vibrancy of their own unique story. This week, we resurrect your inner Wild Woman, summoning her full bloom into this motherhood chapter of your life.

YOU ⌒

Do you sometimes think that the WILD WOMAN in you vanished the instant you became a mother? Well, she didn't. She may have gone underground, but she's there, all right, guiding you with her primal mother-instincts while she waits for an invitation to *howl at the moon*.

Don't make her wait any longer! Being a woman is a multifaceted journey filled with abundant riches. You do not have to give up your Wild Woman in order to claim motherhood. You get to own both, and so much more. So make friends with the Wild Woman inside yourself again. Court her back into your life, so that you can return to the *roots of freedom* that form the matrix of who you truly are.

Resurrecting your inner Wild Woman allows you to tap that free-spirited side of you that lives in the bones of all women. You come from a long line of magical women who created life and embodied the pulse of Mother Earth herself. You can embrace this ancestral inheritance, releasing some control over your daily duties and schedules to drop in and say hello to that powerful, ancient woman within you who may want to dance under the stars, play in the ocean, talk to the animals, and sometimes just let her hair down.

YOUR SOUL ⌒

The soul of a woman is, in its purest form, *untamed.* Sometimes the transition from maiden to mother can trigger a real sense of loss, as your physical freedom is exchanged for the treasures of motherhood. While it is important to acknowledge your feelings and even to mourn the maiden you left behind, you can still access *soul-freedom* anytime you want! Visiting the wildlands within prevents the mundane details of life from overshadowing the magic and mystery of your soul. And feeding your inner Wild Woman with prayer, song, and dance liberates her to color the world with her bold strokes and vital beauty.

YOUR CHILD ᨏ

Every little being that comes earth side is inherently a WILD CHILD and, if allowed to live in a state of personal freedom, may grow to understand the importance of keeping a piece of that Wild-Child spirit alive and well fed. Our children are avatars of freedom—they naturally follow their desire to live every moment with passion, emotion, creativity, and wild abandon!

Honor this wildfire in your children, and feed it a steady diet of beauty, old tales, wild places, and free time. Taming the heart's desire for the wild side of our human nature only makes us grow up wanting to seek it out in desperate and sometimes dangerous ways. Our energy is far better spent living and loving it—all along the way.

REFLECTIONS ᨏ

Do you feel that your wild side is alive and well fed? If not, what prevents you from revitalizing that part of yourself? Are you showing up for yourself in ways that allow you to let your hair down and be wild from time to time, or have you abandoned your inner Wild Woman without even realizing it? This week, spend some time reflecting on this deep, ancient soul of womanhood, and honoring any untamed inclinations that could allow you to access the free spirit that lives within.

SACRED MOTHERHOOD PRACTICE ᨏ

RETURN TO THE WILD. This week, step out of the house and into the wild. Spend time each day singing, praying, howling, creating, or dancing in nature. Connect to the mother source of your untamed spirit.

IDEAS ℰ⁓

- LET YOUR HAIR DOWN. As a mom, you may spend a lot of time with your hair up just because it's easier to fulfill the daily tasks without hair in the way. But this week, literally "let your hair down." Maybe even take a trip to a salon, to refresh your look or add a little splash of color. Do whatever it takes to feel the beauty of freedom!

- COURT THE WILD WOMAN. Gather some sisters, and plan a special outing to feed your wild tribe: Gather together and sing. Pull out the face paints and decorate yourselves as Wild Women. Hit the town for a night of dancing. Tell stories around a fire. And be sure to end the evening with a rousing howl at the moon!

PAIRINGS ℰ⁓

- Book: *Women Who Run with the Wolves* by Clarissa Pinkola Estés
- Music: "Ribbons Undone" by Tori Amos, and "Let Your Hair Down" by MAGIC!

Wild Motherhood

Explore what *wild* means to you. What does your wild side look like? What feeds your inner Wild Woman? Take some time to write about any feelings of loss you may have had since becoming a mother, understanding that to grieve your freedom is to honor the Wild Woman within you. Finally, what will you do this week to unleash your Wild Woman?

Adventure

answering the call

In spring there is a need, a stirring, a summoning—to be fully awake and invested in the quickening of new life and new beginnings. Newborn foals rise up on shaky legs, minutes after birth, eager to set off down the trail without a thought to where it may lead. They remind us that adventure is the path, never the destination. Where are you in your journey? Is adventure on your map?

YOU ℮⁀

Respond to every call that excites your spirit.
—RUMI

Motherhood is an adventure that takes you down many winding roads. It is filled with the side trips of daily tasks, but there is more—always more. Each child you birth has a soul map with a lifetime of opportunities for living out a grand destiny. You play a pivotal role in these destinies, but that does not make up the sum total of who you are. You too have a sacred mission to carry out in this life. Your little beings are a huge part of your adventure, but you may want, need, and seek more. Acknowledging this is OKAY!

When your children are young, you can find freedom in small spaces that appear throughout the day—when your baby is sleeping, or when your partner takes your child out for a walk. In these moments, you can live your adventure no matter where you are on the continuum of your greater vision. This may mean simply reading a book that takes you to distant lands, or planning a daytrip for your family, or even birthing a new home business.

Whatever adventure is calling you, it is important that you overcome fear or stagnation, and answer with a Sacred YES by taking even one significant step, however small.

YOUR SOUL ℮⁀

Mothers are the soul of the home. This is a role that carries deep responsibility, and can be tough to navigate. There are so many unknowns on this grand adventure! But when you open yourself to "not knowing," you often receive answers in spades. Being a mother does not close down your choices or options in the world; it expands them. So it is important to listen closely and with curiosity for what wants to happen next on your journey of motherhood, remembering that you may hear a *call to adventure* beyond your home. As your children grow, that call may get louder and louder, and if you do not respond you may be denying your truest destiny.

When you eventually say YES to whatever awaits, you will teach your children something incredibly valuable—how to receive and respond to the soul's calling. Walking this path of adventure, you can trust that your feet will take you where you need to be; you will meet whomever you are meant to meet; and you will learn lessons that will enhance who you are in the world.

YOUR CHILD

Every moment of a child's life is an adventure. She can transform a cardboard box into a ship that takes her to far-off seas, with a stuffed whale swimming kindly beside the boat to suddenly save her from a mean wooden shark that appears on the other side of the box. This boundless, fifteen-minute epic happens multiple times each day in the lives of children when we allow them the space, the materials, and the encouragement to seek it out.

Adventure lives large within the imagination, but takes real form in us when we act it, live it, breathe it, and become it. Children's adventures are a tonic for the mundane. They are bright arrows shot forth into the vast world of possibilities. We can learn and grow by following in their farsighted footsteps.

REFLECTIONS

What does adventure mean to you? There are many types of adventures in life—personal, emotional, physical, spiritual, and mystical. While these are all unique, they share one key ingredient—*your willingness to trust, and jump off the cliff!*

Think about it: Every adventure—getting married, having a baby, starting a business, or traveling to far off places—contains an element of *letting go.* Every quest starts at a pivotal moment where fear cannot triumph; courage must win, in order to let the wandering begin.

SACRED MOTHERHOOD PRACTICE ☙

GET OUT OF THE RUT. Pick something *new* to do with your family each day this week—and just do it! Try a new recipe, find a new park, pick a new route to school, or just get in the car and drive without a destination in mind, stopping wherever your heart is called.

IDEAS ☙

- START A TRAVEL JAR. Find and decorate a jar to hold slips of paper or maps with the names of all the places that you want to visit with your family—anywhere and everywhere! Add affirmations, images, loose change, and good vibes. Make an unbreakable vow to manifest these travel dreams. And, start planning the first adventure *now!*

- CHOOSE YOUR OWN ADVENTURE. Describe five imaginary lives that you would like to lead. Begin with "I am a …" and see where it takes you. Remember, anything is possible! Notice how you feel. Is there one alternate life that especially calls to you? Perhaps this points to your next adventure.

PAIRINGS ☙

- Book: *The Art of Pilgrimage: The Seeker's Guide to Making Travel Sacred* by Phil Cousineau
- Music: "The Littlest Birds" by The Be Good Tanyas

What adventure would you embark upon if you knew you could not fail (or take a wrong turn)? Write it all out here!

Animal Guides

kinship with all life

As the sap rises and spring stirs in the earth beneath your feet, your animal nature calls. *In response, take a walk on the wild side to see what messages the animals may have for you. Animals in both the Earthly and spiritual realms carry healing gifts, and these are revealed when you open yourself to the circles of kinship that surround you in the natural world.*

YOU ℮⁓

To connect with the animal kingdom, you must first connect with your own animal nature. For me, giving birth was the closest I have ever come to tapping the raw, animalistic power that dwells inside. The guttural sounds, the heightened instincts, the protective embrace of my newborn—all made me feel like a mama bear.

When have you experienced the wisdom and strength of your inner animal? Do your kids think you have superpower vision like an owl, because nothing escapes your watchful eye? Or do you feel most in touch with your animal kin when you are gliding through the ocean waves like a playful dolphin, or basking in the sun like a regal cat?

No matter which animals you relate to most, the inherent beauty and balance of nature are gifts you can receive from the winged ones, the four-legged ones, the swimmers, and the crawlers. Whenever you feel off-kilter, consider a retreat to where the wild things are. Take a walk down the beach or up a mountain to restore your equilibrium, and then notice which animals are present. How do their characteristics reflect aspects of your life as a mother? Do you need to summon the gentleness of a deer, or the playfulness of a dolphin—or are you running from something like a rabbit?

YOUR SOUL ℮⁓

Spring is a time to set aside disbelief and honor every living being as a teacher. Animal medicine is a Native American practice rooted in a deep connection to Spirit and all life. It recognizes the power of animals to heal mind, body, and spirit through their essential natures.

When an animal crosses your path, either as a symbol or in actual physical form, be curious about what balancing, strengthening, or empowering message it may have for you. For example, if you are sitting with your child outside and a hummingbird alights on a branch nearby, perhaps you are being guided to pay attention to your relationship with joy. Or if you are startled by a snake more than once in the course of a week, it could be a sign that transformation is afoot, and it is time to shed an old way of being. This week, pay careful attention to the animals that appear to you, whether along a forested path, in a deck of *Medicine Cards,* or in a dream. Be reverent and open to their guidance.

YOUR CHILD ☙

Nurturing your children's relationship to animals fosters their own special kinship with all life. Children often have "a way" with animals. These innocents instinctively know how to connect with animals using emotional, physical, and spiritual awareness. By allowing your children to independently develop this way of relating not only teaches them to be caring and compassionate, it also supports their own well-being.

While being on a farm may conjure images of an idyllic childhood, a flock of backyard chickens or even a beloved cat can also connect your children to the cycle of life, and teach them to forge bonds with other beings. You can also invite your children for regular walks in the woods. Here you can put on your keen owl eyes and sensitive deer ears to find the animal sisters and brothers hiding nearby. Look carefully and listen deeply to help your children attune to the animal's essence and be nurtured by this good medicine.

REFLECTIONS ☙

Our connection to animal wisdom arises from the recognition that *we are all connected;* we have within us a part of the divine and a part of all other beings. We are not alone. The Lakota prayer *mitakuye oyasin,* meaning "all my relations," reminds us that we can draw inspiration and insight from the whole family of creation.

SACRED MOTHERHOOD PRACTICE ❧

CALL IN YOUR ANIMAL GUIDES. Ask for a dream—or trust your intuition—to identify a spirit-animal guide for yourself and each of your children. When you or a child needs support or protection, visualize the spirit animal keeping watch and guiding the way.

IDEAS ❧

- HONOR YOUR ANIMAL ALLIES. Place symbolic representations—images, bones, or poems—of your family's spirit animals on your altar. Then offer them prayers of kinship and gratitude in your morning practice.
- FOLLOW THE WAY OF THE ANIMALS. Tracking with your kids is a fun way to get to know the characteristics of your animal kin. Grab a tracking book and spend time crawling on the ground, looking for bent blades of grass and examining pawprints to awaken your latent animal instincts!

PAIRINGS ❧

- Book: *Medicine Cards: The Discovery of Power Through the Ways of Animals* by Jamie Sams and David Carson
- Children's book: *Children's Spirit Animal Cards* by Steven D. Farmer

journal on

Animal Guides

Do you have a strong affinity for a particular animal? Dig deeper to understand why this animal has presented itself to you. How does it show up in your life? How might it serve as a reminder of a gift that you carry—leadership, intuition, or loyalty, for instance? How can it help you meet your challenges as a mother?

_____

_____

_____

_____

_____

_____

_____

_____

_____

_____

_____

_____

Summer

Ocean

Inner Child

Innocence

Emotions

Dirt

Sticky

Watermelon

The Senses

Embodiment

Freedom

Instinct

Sexuality

Popsicles

Fear

Red–Hot Love

The Present Moment

Nurturing

Wonder

Trust

Crust

in the flow

In the summertime spirit of letting go while basking in the warm breezes, cooling off in the rolling waves, and reviving the innocence of childhood, this week looks to the roots of trust, as you begin understanding your own flow.

YOU ☙

"Trust" is a big word! When much of life is spent in unconscious fear and a scarcity mentality, it can be hard to surrender and "go with the flow." To do so, you must tap a profound sense of trust. As a mama, you probably work hard trying to make all the pieces fall into place; perhaps you tend to come unraveled when it seems things are not going the way you planned or expected—when in reality you simply are not seeing the big picture, the cosmic unfolding in which everything works out in the end. And what if it doesn't? Well then, it's not the end!

Motherhood can seem hopelessly challenging and bleak when you struggle against the flow of your life. Alternately, when you trust that you have enough, and that following your heart-path will allow things to unfold optimally, you will be rewarded with abundance and grace. Many gifts will be laid upon your doorstep. You must pick up these gifts, nurture them, grow them into your dreams—and then give them back to the world. This keeps you in the flow.

YOUR SOUL ☙

When you live in a place of TRUST, you are in the flow of universal energy. Life appears to unfold in magical ways that support the heart-path you are meant to follow. This doesn't mean everything is easy. But it does mean that when challenges arise, you can reshape your thoughts, and learn to see rough patches as just a part of the bigger plan.

This is when it gets hard, Mama. How can you be okay when things don't turn out the way you think they should? *Trust* that there is a grand design for you to realize your highest potential, and to serve the greater good for your children and the world. This faith will anchor you in your own personal spiritual flow, keeping you completely in sync with the universe. Now, that is some awesome mama power!

YOUR CHILD ⌒

Harness that mama power to hold space for the sometimes-difficult truth that while your children came into this world through you, they do not belong to you. Your children have their own dance in life. Sometimes you may try to shape their destinies with your own desires, but ultimately you must trust the flow of their lives even when it differs from your plans.

When you understand that each child has a *unique* part to play in the universal fabric of life, you can release your attachments to how you think things should be, and trust that everything will unfold exactly as it is meant to unfold. You are here to guide and help your children, but not control them. You are the steady bow from which these sweet arrows are shot forth into the world. Trust them to fly on their own and land where they may.

REFLECTIONS ⌒

Spend some time unraveling the mystery of trust in your life. In mothering my four children, I have found it difficult to surrender and trust their inclinations, and even my own. It can be painful to watch your children fall and make mistakes. You instinctively want to protect them from every little thing that could possibly go wrong. Rest assured that, when you place trust in yourself and in your path as a mother, you will know when to guide your children and when to let it all *flow*.

SACRED MOTHERHOOD PRACTICE ⌒

MAKE A VOW. Right here and now, commit to saying, "I HAVE ENOUGH! I AM ENOUGH!" and "I AM FULLY SUPPORTED BY SPIRIT!" Make your daily meditation about trusting the path you are on, trusting your mothering flow of energy, and trusting that there are lessons in everything you are experiencing. Look for the lessons, and the beauty in each lesson—*especially the hard ones!*

IDEAS ⌒

- CREATE TRUST TOUCHSTONES. Go on a nature walk with your family, and ask each person to find a stone that calls to him or her—

trust that you've all chosen the perfect ones. Take the stones home, and decorate them with the word "trust." Keep these touchstones on your altar or in another sacred space, and hold one in your hand whenever you fall back into a place of fear or lack. Invite your children to do the same.

· SURRENDER TO A DIFFERENT FLOW. One day this summer, set aside your own schedule and routines, and empower your children to determine the flow. Be open to *whatever* wants to unfold. You may spend the entire day sitting in a tree in your pajamas, or come home from the beach long after dark and have ice cream for dinner. There is wisdom in whimsy, and it is quite possible that something completely unexpected—and truly marvelous!—may happen.

· MAKE AN ENERGY-BALANCER SPRAY. To help you stay in your own flow, mix up this spritzer and use it to rebalance your energy through the day.

ENERGY-BALANCER SPRAY

(Compliments of Lety Murphy from the Sacred Scent program)

2 oz. distilled water

2 oz. 80-proof alcohol

3 drops cedarwood essential oil

1 drop vetiver essential oil

4 drops sweet orange essential oil

3 drops clove essential oil

Mix all ingredients in a four-ounce spray bottle, and spritz yourself as needed.

---

pairings ☙

· Children's book: *Zen Shorts* by Jon J. Muth

· Music: "Here, Down on My Knees" by Nina Lee

journal on

Trust

Describe your current relationship to TRUST. How has it ebbed
and flowed through your life? What
would it take for you to fully surrender to divine grace?

Embodiment

*what makes you
come alive?*

As the weeks unfold and summer begins to bear the fruits of your labors, it is time to explore the range of your embodiment. How is Sacred Motherhood manifesting in your life? Do you inhabit yourself more fully? Are you living your potential? This is the moment to touch down in your body, and celebrate your ALIVENESS!

YOU ⌾

During the mothering years, there are days (pray there are not too many!) when you wake up and merely "go through the motions." Perhaps you are sleep-deprived, or your mind has taken you away to a sunnier paradise. Whatever the reason, you get dressed, pack the lunches, drive to work—but never really land fully in your body, or in your life. Scary, right?

Luckily, there are also euphoric moments, such as giving birth or making love, that drop you back into your body and remind you what it means to be alive. What would it be like to spend more time in this fully embodied state?

For each of us, the doorway to embodiment is unique. How do you access your *joie de vivre*? In your joyful aliveness, what are you embodying? What one-of-a-kind expression of the divine are you manifesting through your being? Are you an artist, a lover, a farmer, a mother? Do not be afraid to be ALL that you are. Don't hide, or be small. Feed life itself with your movement, your creations, *and* your magnificent failures. What your children (and the world) need is for you to be FULLY alive.

YOUR SOUL ⌾

Often a spiritual path is misunderstood as a departure from the physical realm, in favor of a reunion with the spiritual realm. But you are actually a spiritual being who signed up to incarnate. You are here on Earth to experience the lusciousness of being embodied, on whatever path you choose. This life itself is DIVINE!

If escape is what you are seeking, you may be avoiding connection with your body, perhaps in an attempt to transcend trauma, illness, or some other form of disempowerment. Tread softly in this exploration, and seek healing experiences such as psychotherapy, bodywork, or a spiritual retreat that can allow you to retrieve and reclaim those parts that have been wounded and estranged. The path of embodiment is the path of wholeness.

YOUR CHILD ❧

Offering your child a holistic childhood means tending to the vitality of MIND, BODY, AND SPIRIT. By turning your attention toward embodiment, you can nurture all three. Childhood is a time to climb, jump, run, swing, and spin. Not only is this movement fun (albeit tiring for mamas), it supports healthy brain development, builds a strong physical foundation for growth, and encourages the soul to wholly incarnate. Make room for your child to move freely and express all of who he is, including the bigness and the loudness. Also notice how your child's body changes almost daily, yet his embodied nature—his essence—remains the same. Bless this eternal spark that enlivens what you love.

REFLECTIONS ❧

As a mother, dive into the fullness and suppleness of your body—a vessel that sustains life. Not only did your body support the miraculous growth of a new human, it enabled another soul to incarnate. Your body is thus a vehicle of embodiment for both yourself and your children. Beyond birth, your children will always remind you of the goddess-like gifts a mother's body bestows. They forever crave your life-giving touch, your love-infused cooking, and your welcoming lap.

SACRED MOTHERHOOD PRACTICE ❧

EMBODY YOURSELF IN THE NOW. To inhabit deeper layers of your embodied presence, start with where you are, in this moment: Tune into your body. Where do you feel the flow of vital energy, and where do you feel blocked? What you resist persists, so hone your nonjudgmental awareness to focus on any areas of tension or discomfort. As you breathe into the sensation, notice how it begins to shift, open, and integrate. Allow your body to be your guide toward wholeness.

IDEAS ☙

· TAKE A PLUNGE. There is nothing like cold water to bring you into your body! When you are overthinking something, or feel bleary-eyed, hightail it to a river, lake, or ocean, strip down, and jump in. Feel the energy surge in your body, and take pleasure in feeling so full of life.

· TAKE A DANCE BREAK. Put some music on, and allow the rhythm to awaken every cell in your body. Don't worry about how you look, or whether you're dancing to the beat. Just practice listening to your body and moving in any way that pleases you. Dance to express ALL that you embody—love, grief, joy, sorrow—everything! Alone, with a partner, staccato, or groovy—dancing shifts energy like nothing else. Motherhood is a time to BUST A MOVE!

PAIRINGS ☙

· Children's song: "Miracle" by Renee Toback

· Food: CHOCOLATE!

· Music: "Existence" by Shylah Ray Sunshine, and "Woman (Oh Mama)" by Joy Williams

What makes you come alive? Write it below. What, if anything, is keeping you from living this full expression of your being? Write this down too.

Now experiment with turning these limitations around, and reshaping them into prayers. For example, "My partner is challenging my ability to be fully alive" might become, "I am in partnership with all that is alive within myself."

The Beauty Way

it's the only way

What is more beautiful than the sun setting over the ocean, or stars glistening in the sky on a clear night? The natural beauty that surrounds us is an inspirational backdrop to life, and feeds our souls in ways that nothing else can. Summertime provides the perfect opportunity for us to explore, create, and land smack-dab in the middle of BEAUTY. *In order for beauty to transform us, we must see it, experience it, and appreciate it. As Cheryl Strayed reminds us in* Wild, *"There's a sunrise and a sunset every day, and you can choose to be there for it. You can put yourself in the way of beauty."*

YOU ❧

If you look closely enough, there is deep beauty in everything. Beauty is what ultimately soothes the soul, and balances the light and shadow that exist in all things. When you are surrounded by physical manifestations of beauty—flowers on the table, a rainbow after a storm, or waves crashing on a beach—you are naturally inspired, and *you feel good.* To spread this kind of wonderfulness in the world, follow the BEAUTY WAY!

The Beauty Way is a path and a practice devoted to the beauty in all things. It is a commitment to share your golden truth every chance you get; to create a lovely, nurturing environment for your family that supports living at a high vibration; and—most of all—to offer your generosity, kindness, and good nature to everyone you meet.

The true essence of beauty is not defined by certain physical attributes. Rather, it's about how you give your gifts to the world, how you intentionally choose to inspire others. The beauty that lives inside you can be expressed in simple gestures—wiping a tear off your child's cheek, sharing a glance of acknowledgment, or even smiling at a stranger. Living the Beauty Way brings consciousness to the effect you have on others, and asks you to share your radiant heart by creating as many uplifting, enlivening moments as you can.

YOUR SOUL ❧

Living the Beauty Way also calls for opening yourself to experience the beauty all around you. Be on the lookout for moments in which you might collide with beauty and inspiration! Sometimes this means feeding your soul a Beauty-Way helping of inspiration with a clean home, a walk in nature, a trip to the flea market, a new skein of yarn, or a few hours in the kitchen cooking a meal full of love for your family. Other times, you will stumble upon an unexpected Beauty-Way moment. Maybe you'll be walking down the street and notice a stone with "You are beautiful!" written on it, or look up from your late-night deskwork to glimpse the full moon peeking out from behind the clouds.

There will also be times when saying YES to the Beauty Way means using a Holy NO. A long while ago, I stopped watching violent movies because I could feel them penetrating my soul in ways that did not feel good. It occurred to me that if I would not allow my children to watch soul-sabotaging media, why would I subject myself to it? To follow the Beauty Way, we must seek out experiences that feed our souls with light and love, and that we can then share with our families and the world.

YOUR CHILD ⌖

Children are one of the purest manifestations of beauty in the world—they are the heart and soul of it all. The essence and innocence of childhood reflects the divinity in each of us, and should be protected as long as possible. Discovering the darker side of the world can be reserved for later years. For now, allow your children to be immersed in the simple beauty that will unfold their true nature. Here are a few ways that you can bring beauty into your children's lives:

- Let children use glasses, cloth napkins, and real dinnerware with their meals, to create a family table full of beauty. They do not need to use plastic just because they are learning. They can follow in your footsteps and learn to care gently for delicate items. It's okay if something gets broken—that's part of life. Adults break stuff too!

- Shower some attention on your children's rooms. Ultimately, when children feel good in their spaces, their emotions can be navigated with more ease, and they can express their beauty-filled hearts. Invite them to create small flower arrangements for their bedside tables. Fill their rooms with pleasant scents using an essential-oil diffuser or mild incense. Add twinkle lights or a soft lamp to diffuse harsh overhead light.

· Invite your child to join you in leaving every place you visit more beautiful than it was when you found it: Pick up a piece of trash in the park. Bring a bouquet to school. Straighten crooked pictures on Grandma's walls.

REFLECTIONS ⌒◡

How has beauty played a role in your life up until now? Growing up, was your home filled with loving vibrations that you could see, feel, and touch? Was it filled with fresh flowers and the smells of home cooking? Or was it filled with clutter, noise, and anger? How do you want to shape your own children's experiences of beauty?

SACRED MOTHERHOOD PRACTICE ⌒◡

PUT A SMILE IN YOUR PRACTICE. Smile at a stranger. Do this several times a day. Not only does it make them feel good, it elevates your vibration, helps you live in more joy, and brings your natural beauty to the world.

IDEAS ⌒◡

· BRING THE BEAUTY WAY HOME. Take a look around. Do you love your home? Is it beautiful *to you?* Is it clean and organized in a way that uplifts you? If not, how can you add some simple beauty to your living space? Think of every space in your home as sacred. Polish each one with your special golden touch of organization and simple nature-inspired gorgeousness.

· LEAVE LOVE-STONES. Choose rocks, and paint positive affirmations on them. The next time you go on a walk, leave them in random places for others to find and be touched by your gift. Have your children help you with the creation and adventure of sharing them in the world. This is one way of teaching them the Beauty Way!

pairings ☙

- Book: *The Way of Beauty: Five Meditations for Spiritual Transformation* by François Cheng
- Music: "Beautiful" by India Arie

journal on

The Beauty Way ❦

What does beauty mean to you? Is it how you look, how you feel, what you create, what you do for a living, or how you share your light with the world? How can you create more profound Beauty-Way moments in your home and in the world?

Nurture

filling your cup

Summer's soft breezes and relaxed schedules create an atmosphere of generosity and ease in which to cradle your children and yourself. As your nurturing-mama arms embrace and care for those around you, do not forget to hold your own JOY *and* GROWTH *as sacred.*

YOU ⌾⟀

"If Mama ain't happy, ain't nobody happy." Though trite, this phrase conveys well-worn wisdom. It points to the importance of self-nurturance in the throes of motherhood. Easier said than done! The mother-martyr archetype is alive and well within most of us—she'd skip a meal to grocery-shop for the family. She'd forgo exercise to run the kids to soccer practice. Yet we all know that when we neglect our own well-being, *everyone* suffers the consequences.

This week, make a promise to FILL YOUR CUP until it overflows, in order to water those around you. Motherhood is never-ending, so don't wait for the perfect, spacious moment to arrive. Let go of all guilt so that you can manifest the space and time that you need for self-care. And then be sure to follow through, even if your toddler has a meltdown as you head out the door.

You are doing this for *yourself!* Own it. It's okay—your children will reap the benefits. By nurturing yourself, you are teaching your children the importance of loving and caring for oneself. Pray they follow in your footsteps!

YOUR SOUL ⌾⟀

As you step up to tend to your own needs and moods as a woman as well as a mother, look beyond the band-aid indulgences that help you keep it all together—your morning latte, retail therapy, or chocolate, for instance—and seek out experiences that deeply nurture your soul. These might be as simple as a walk on the beach that activates your bliss, or as in-depth as a meditation retreat that gets you back onto your cushion.

If you don't have a perfect antidote to burnout at your fingertips, consider unearthing former passions currently buried under the responsibilities of motherhood. When you were younger, did you come alive on horseback? Perhaps it is time to get back in the saddle. And what about dancing? If you find it impossible to get to a club these days, seek out a 5Rhythms or Nia dance/fitness class—or simply create a solo dance party in your living room.

Mothering is a transformational experience, so you also may need to conjure fresh ideas for personal renewal. Listen to what your soul is longing for *right now!*

YOUR CHILD ⌒

As a mother, you may feel that nurturing children fills the better part of your life. Yet we all know there are days when true nurturance eludes us. You have nothing to give if you are running on empty. When you take time out for yourself and return feeling full, you can again shower your child with warmth and welcome.

One way to deeply nurture your child's whole being is to indulge the senses. For babies and toddlers, breastfeeding is the touchstone multisensory treat. As children grow up, the homey smell of warm cookies, the pleasing vision of fresh flowers, the healing taste of chicken soup, the tender touch of a goodbye kiss, or the soothing sound of a favorite lullaby may come to epitomize comfort, especially when these experiences are expressions of a mother's love. What nurturing rituals lie at the heart of your home? How might you tap the rich sensory field—reaching all of the senses—to offer simple, beautiful, and natural nurturance for yourself and yours?

REFLECTIONS ⌒

If you are having a hard time with the idea of nurturing yourself, you may be bumping up against an old, perhaps unconscious belief that you are not worthy. This is true for many women, including myself. Hold yourself tenderly as you work to rewrite this script. Write yourself a love letter acknowledging that you are inherently good, and ultimately divine. Give yourself abundant props, praise, and love. *You deserve it!*

SACRED MOTHERHOOD PRACTICE ⌒

NURTURE YOURSELF AND YOUR SISTERS WITH A MOTHER HONORING. Invite a few friends to spend an afternoon of giving and receiving. Make a flower crown, and a comfortable throne. Each mama is given a turn in the seat of honor, soaking her feet in a footbath of flower petals and essential oils while her sisters massage her feet, hands, legs, and shoulders; brush her hair; feed her chocolate; whisper affirmations in her ear; and sing to her. Make the experience as loving and over-the-top delicious as possible.

IDEAS ⌒

- TAKE A BATH. First create a sanctuary of warmth and beauty around your tub. Bring in flowers, and a sea of candles. Make the bath as full and hot as possible. Add dried flowers, soaking salts, and essential oils. Then be sure to give yourself enough time to luxuriate in the water!

- CREATE A SPA DAY TO PAMPER YOUR LITTLE ONES. Offer footbaths and backrubs to your children. Brush and braid their hair. And have fun making an edible facial mask with natural ingredients from your kitchen such as avocado, banana, plain yogurt, honey, and chocolate. You can even bust out the cucumber-slices-on-the-eyes for an ultimate spa experience!

PAIRINGS ⌒

- Herbal Ally: Lavender soothes and refreshes the mind, body and spirit. Place 2–3 drops of lavender essential oil in your cupped palms and inhale the scent, or rub a few drops onto your temples or the bottoms of feet.

- Sacred Living Movement Retreat: Sacred Self-Love (online)

journal on

Nurture

Plan a full day of nurturing just for
you. Make it bold, and *beautiful!*

_____

_____

_____

_____

_____

_____

_____

_____

_____

_____

_____

_____

_____

_____

_____

_____

_____

_____

_____

Sacred Play

*awakening your
inner child*

Summer is practically synonymous with play. Children eagerly await summer's invitation to a carefree frolic from breakfast until they fall into bed long after dinner. These long, expansive days beckon you too. Your inner child stirs. This week, seize every opportunity to join your child in the summertime world of sacred play. Magic and wonder are in store.

YOU ⟲⌣

Play is a child's "work," but for a mama it can be hard to justify the time off for pure, unadulterated fun. Be assured that when you get down on the floor and play with your child, the value lies in simply abandoning your agenda to arrive in the present moment. Play unfolds, *play-by-play*. There is no plotting or planning. Even when grand plans are the game of the day—when your eight-year-old undertakes to build an airplane that actually flies, and you want to help—adult blueprints and linear timelines can derail the magic of possibility.

Allowing imagination to rule the outcome of a few precious hours—better yet, an entire day—can deliver a welcome relief and an unforeseen boon. Not only does play release endorphins and stress, promote vitality and well-being, and stimulate the brain and creativity for you and your child, it strengthens the bond you share, and channels joy into your relationship.

Need more convincing? In reminding us to expect and even relish the unexpected, play also serves as a sacred clown, lightening things up when you start to take yourself too seriously. *Amen!*

YOUR SOUL ⟲⌣

With all this in mind, resist the temptation to plan away your summer days. Instead, fall into the timelessness of play. Play comes easier for some of us than others. Are you a Peter Pan parent who steps effortlessly into Neverland as if you never left? Or did this make-believe realm recede as the adult world of relationships and productivity offered up a new landscape? If so, it can be difficult to find the way back—but it is possible!

Follow the trail of breadcrumbs left by your children. Let them rouse your inherent wonder and delight by beholding the world from their perspective. The sky does not have to be blue; pigs can talk; and mud pies can taste delicious. This journey into childhood promises to reawaken your inner child in all her myriad forms—Wounded Child, Divine Child, Innocent Child, and Trickster. Each archetype can be stimulated, explored, and healed as you play alongside your child. Whether or not your younger years were idyllic, motherhood offers an opportunity to recreate a happy childhood for yourself—and *pay it forward.*

YOUR CHILD ⚲⌒⌐

In a culture that values product over process, it is easy to overlook the importance of unstructured, open-ended play, where children inhabit a world that they discover and create moment-to-moment. This is the type of play children especially love—as they should. There is ample evidence pointing to the crucial role of free play in wiring the brain to learn, move, think, relate, and create—essentially, to live.

To inspire play that stimulates creative movement and imagination, think about how you might provide inviting, sensory-rich play environments. For a young child, try setting up a beautiful playspace in your home using open toyshelves with baskets of simple, natural toys like tree-branch blocks, seashells, river rocks, silk scarves, felt animals, and wooden figures. Outside, add some sand or dirt and a little water, for hours of fun. All of these playthings are inexpensive and can become anything the game of the day demands or the imagination desires. Also, when toys are sourced from the natural world or made by your loving hands, they are imbued with feeling, and encourage the integration of the hands, the head, and the heart.

REFLECTIONS ⚲⌒⌐

The lighthearted flow of energy in a playful child is irresistible. Whether this child lives in your home or dwells in your heart, her ability to find magic and merriment in each moment touches everyone. A playful child illuminates the seeds of joy and love that we all carry—and reminds us to greet the world unburdened and anew, to realize the potential that each day holds.

SACRED MOTHERHOOD PRACTICE ◌〜

ENLIGHTEN YOUR PRACTICE WITH PLAY. Although children become more absorbed in play without adult intervention, set aside ten minutes a day to enter into your child's play world, just for your own soul's sake. Practice following your child's lead rather than directing. Above all, be silly, laugh freely, and let your imagination run wild.

IDEAS ◌〜

- INSTITUTE FAMILY GAME NIGHT. One night a week, pull out the board games, have a pick-up basketball game, or commence an amusing game of charades. Although a little healthy competition can be fun, there are also many cooperative games out there to help you actualize the saying, "The family that plays together stays together."

- REIMAGINE YOUR CHILD'S PLAYSPACE. Move the play area out of your child's bedroom and into the center of the home, where she can feel your grounding presence. Make it beautiful too, with rich colors and natural materials. Keep it simple, with a few, well-chosen, imaginative toys, and baskets to keep them organized. Rotate playthings occasionally to keep them fresh. And be sure to set some guidelines to encourage collaboration and keep it fun for everyone.

PAIRINGS ◌〜

- Crystal: Amber is a chakra-balancing stone that fills your body and mind with spiritual energy that supports joy and lightheartedness.

journal on

Sacred Play

Describe your Inner Child. What enlivens her? What scares her? What comforts her? And how does she like to *play*?

_____

_____

_____

_____

_____

_____

_____

_____

_____

_____

_____

_____

Get Dirty!

days well played

Mud pies, popsicle-sticky faces, watermelon juice hands, sand-covered feet, explosions of paint, glue, and glitter, and couch-cushion forts are sweet visions of summertime's messy play. When your kids come into the house covered from head to toe in dirt, you know it's been a great day of play and experience for them. Allowing dirt-inspired play to happen for your children also expands your own willingness to step into messy freedom without worrying about what the neighbors (or anyone else) will think.

YOU ☙

Welcome the summer months as a time to dig into the freedom that nature-play and gardening offer, and embrace the simple teachings of the Earth. In other words, GET DIRTY!

Does this idea make you cringe, or cheer? How do you feel about allowing dirty messes to happen in your life? Do you get stressed out when your children are elbow-deep in mud with dirt caked under their nails, or do you celebrate their dirt-streaked faces as a part of a day well played?

When you are willing to risk a little muck and grime, the Earth offers up her elemental wisdom. In the garden, on the beach, or around the campfire, teachings in patience, freedom, creativity, transformation, and stewardship abound. But messes are not limited to the great outdoors; they sneak inside too, and can transform the living room in an instant! But what then?

YOUR SOUL ☙

Indoors or out, getting dirty lies at the heart of *allowing*. It forces us to relinquish control over everything that may or may not happen. Only then can we truly understand that our little ones need free space in order to develop into well-rounded people. Opening more to the messiness of childhood allows magic to alight in your home for both your children and your soul. However, although this is very good medicine, it can be a hard pill to swallow.

If this is true for you, take baby steps. See what happens when you crawl into one of your children's couch-cushion forts. Maybe you will never want to leave! Or maybe you'll be inspired to add some twinkle lights to make it more enchanting, even if your tidy house suffers. There is always time and space to *clean it up later!*

YOUR CHILD ✑

Encourage your children to get dirty! Ask them to join you in the garden, where they can dig in the earth, sowing seeds that they can water and tend over the summer months. They can plant pumpkins to carve for Halloween, or plant a pizza garden full of special herbs and ingredients—and then create a pizza party with their friends. Inviting a child into the wonders of growing something from nothing instills a lifelong love and respect for the Earth in a way that nothing else can. After all, real-life encounters are what solidify teachings and help us integrate them into our bodies, minds, and spirits.

I once saw a family walking on a beautiful, tantalizing beach in Kauai. The kids all had to keep their tennis shoes on, even though they were begging to get their toes in the sand. The well-meaning mama kept saying the sand was too hot. Even if the sand is hot, *allow* your children to experience it for themselves. It won't really hurt them, and they stand to gain more understanding and appreciation for Mother Earth.

REFLECTIONS ✑

How far can you go to release control and encourage children to explore freely? I have a child who never wants to wear shoes, *anywhere!* I allow him to go barefoot most of the time. It's not always easy, and sometimes folks disapprove, but I believe this is his way of staying connected to the Earth and nature, which is his passion. Perhaps we mamas should take our own bare feet out for walks more often, so that we can also connect with Mother Earth, and experience her powerful care and support.

SACRED MOTHERHOOD PRACTICE ❧

Get dirty! This week, make a vow to say YES to the mess. Each day, look the other way when harmless fun is exploding all over the kitchen, or invite your children to join you in a really messy art project (think papier-mâché, or Jackson Pollock), or plant some beauty in a little patch of earth. When you are all done, you can make cleanup time part of the fun by keeping it light and joyful.

IDEAS ❧

- CREATE A GARDEN WITH YOUR CHILDREN. Whether small or large, your garden can be home to anything—flowers, herbs, fruits, or veggies. Getting dirty while growing beauty and food is a wonderful way for everyone to experience the miracles of Mother Earth. And the watering, weeding, and harvesting will keep you coming back for more and more experiences with dirt.

- SLEEP UNDER THE STARS. Pitch a tent in your backyard for a little nature-hangout time with your family. You can even bust out the s'mores for some really sticky fun!

PAIRINGS ❧

- Books: *Roots, Shoots, Buckets & Boots: Gardening Together with Children* by Sharon Lovejoy, *Plant Ally Cards* by Lisa McLaughlin, and *I Love Dirt* by Jennifer Ward
- Children's book: *The Story of Frog Belly Rat Bone* by Timothy Basil Ering

Get Dirty!

Journal here about your willingness to *allow* dirty and messy play to
happen around your home. Look
back at your own childhood: Were
you able to spend time really get-
ting dirty? Did you love exploring the treasures of the Earth, and/or
expressing yourself without fear of cleanup time? How can you give
your children the gift of following their imaginations in limitless—and
often messy—ways?

_____

_____

_____

_____

_____

_____

_____

_____

_____

_____

_____

_____

_____

Two Hands

the art + craft
of motherhood

Summer seduces you into activities that delight the body and the senses. What better season to put your two hands to work creating beauty? Bust out the opposable thumbs this week, and discover the ripple effect of joy when art and craft take center stage.

YOU ❧

With our skillful hands and vibrant imaginations, humans possess the unique ability to create. It is one of the most precious rewards of soulful incarnation. In traditional cultures, handmade creations were essential to survival and quality of life, but they also served as *gifts of beauty* for the enjoyment of the gods. If you have ever dismissed art and craft as frivolous activities, think again, and let your hands lead the way to better living.

Many of motherhood's more pleasurable pursuits involve making things by hand. Why? Scientifically speaking, drawing, painting, sculpting, and handcrafts stimulate the production of mood-related neurotransmitters—*knit and be happy!*

Whether or not you are drawn to creating with your hands, motherhood offers the opportunity to develop this passion with an audience of enthusiasts—namely, your children. At any age, an appropriate art or craft project will open the door to self-expression and mutual fun. As an added bonus, handmade items convey the creativity and love of the maker, thus infusing your home with character and soul.

YOUR SOUL ❧

Chief among the merits of the arts and crafts is the fact that no two sets of hands leave the same mark upon their creations. This singular expression is a signature of the soul. The more you practice your craft, the more you encourage your soul to reveal itself. The same is true for your children when you embolden them to remain faithful to the movement and style in their own fingers.

What might you glimpse, through this lens of awareness, in the rawness and immediacy of your child's latest masterpiece? When you struggle to recognize the genius in your own artwork, or feel frustrated when your child's budding artistry doesn't match your expectations, remember that it is the beautiful imperfections that carry the story of your humanity and invite spirit to feast upon your creative offerings.

YOUR CHILD ⌥

As little hands grapple with knitting needles or dribble a little blue paint over the red to see what happens, neural pathways are being laid. Educating your children's hands in a variety of artistic methods and media not only unlocks the creative potential of their mind—it enlivens their hearts. By exploring material, texture, color, and line, your child is having a conversation with the world. She is taking in all that is unfolding around her, and learning to respond with feeling and form. Whether she is playfully coaxing a lump of clay into the shape of a turtle, or carefully stitching up a length of cloth to make a skirt, she is discovering ways to share her inner landscape and lend her own note to the universal song.

REFLECTIONS ⌥

In your creative dabbling, have you ever wondered why knitting has caught on like wildfire in recent years, and in repeated cycles over the decades? For me, knitting offers a mindfulness practice that I can weave into my daily rhythm. As I knit one, purl two, my mind releases its grip on distracting thoughts and falls into a meditative calm.

I don't need to sneak off to find this inner peace. When knitting with little ones underfoot, I find that my full presence sets a tone for the room. Crafting is actually a classic Waldorf Education strategy for encouraging harmonious play. Teachers busy their hands with mending or polishing, to encourage the children's absorbed and contented play. You might find that it works for you too!

SACRED MOTHERHOOD PRACTICE ⟶

MAKE SOMETHING FOR YOUR CHILD. Even my less crafty friends have found themselves making dolls, or needle-felting puppets, once they have children, so let your child inspire you to activate your hands. Identify one item—a toy, a scarf, doll clothes, a go-cart—that would delight your little one. Instead of heading to the store, settle down to make it with your own two hands. You can invite the little ones to help, and/or watch as you make it.

IDEAS ⟶

- GIVE FROM YOUR HEART AND HANDS. As birthdays roll around, commit to making handmade gifts for family and friends. Stitch a simple birthday crown for your little one, or create an inspirational custom journal for your budding teen. Set your child up with beads or paints to fashion heartfelt presents for their little friends too. Then spread the love by also inviting friends to bring handmade gifts to your family birthday celebrations.

- CREATE AN ART STUDIO. Whether it is a closet, a table, or an entire room, set up a go-to space for busy hands. Outfit it with well-organized tools and materials for a variety of handmade creations. Welcome messes. And visit it often!

PAIRINGS ⟶

- Books: *Crafts Through the Year* by Thomas and Petra Berger and *Handmade Home: Simple Ways to Repurpose Old Materials into New Family Treasures* by Amanda Blake Soule

journal on

Two Hands

What are your hands itching to create? Use this space to sketch out two art or craft projects that pique your interest. Start by freely exploring your inspiration and ideas. Then give some thought to what materials and skills you will need to *make it happen!*

Simplicity

less is more

With relaxed routines and languid days, summer is the season of simple joys.
*There is no better time to adopt the motto "*LESS IS MORE*." Less stuff equals*
more space. Less running around gives you more quality time. Less attachment
means more freedom. This week, simply simplify, slow down, and savor the gifts of
motherhood.

YOU ⌇

Summer holidays sing of freedom and adventure, but also of simplicity. Sneaking away for an annual family holiday at the beach or in the mountains offers a welcome respite from the demands and overburdened habits of daily living. On vacation, it doesn't matter if dinner is an hour late, or if the bathroom faucet needs fixing. Toys are left behind—and not missed!—and a few rumpled shirts and pants qualify as an acceptable wardrobe. For a short time, you leave everything behind; you find that contentment fills the open spaces normally inhabited by tight schedules and insidious accumulation. But how might these tenets of simplicity set the tone in your home throughout the year?

While your weekly rhythm has more complexity and staccato qualities than a free-flowing holiday, many of the ways you fill your home and your hours may in fact be superfluous. Take a look at your wardrobe, for example: Do you wear everything that you own? Or do you have a few favorite outfits stuffed into a closet full of "not quite right" clothing that never sees the light of day?

Imagine how pleasurable getting dressed in the morning could be if you had fewer jeans, but loved them all. Now extend the same possibility to your child's dresser. Could you eliminate the battle over what to wear if there were fewer choices? Four preferred dresses might empower your daughter's self-expression, while fourteen are likely to suffocate her in a wrinkled mess.

YOUR SOUL ⌇

Whether you are thinking about how to reorganize your closets, or strategizing about how to make it through another hectic week, consider simplifying in order to make more room for your soul. Simply put, simplicity allows each experience to blossom wholly and feed you deeply. When you are not racing from one place to another, you can stop to smell the roses. And, when your mind is not racing from one thought to another, you can approach anything from folding laundry to having sex as a mindful and therefore more enjoyable activity.

Counter to our culture of acquisition, the practice of simplicity is not about filling up to achieve happiness. Rather, it is about emptying yourself to receive fulfillment from your naturally arising awareness and the sacredness of your life.

YOUR CHILD ⊜◠◡

Children too thrive in the space of simplicity. Limited choices, fewer toys, and reduced activities may sound like the path of deprivation. On the contrary, this approach allows a child's attention to land fully in each opportunity and mine its riches. Your children have the rest of their lives to juggle packed days and profuse possessions, if they so choose. Childhood is the time to master the precious engagement of their open minds and hearts with each simple, spacious moment.

With this in mind, think of how you might pare down the offerings your child must manage each day. You might, for example, forego the usual complex menu of breakfast options. You could simplify the morning shuffle by offering oatmeal on Monday, eggs on Tuesday, cereal on Wednesday, and so on.

With shelves of books that go unread, you might try creating a rotating library that spotlights ten books at a time while the others rest in a closet. As an alternative to buying more toys for your child's entertainment, try hiding a few at a time that you can reintroduce when interests shift and the moment is ripe. And finally, reevaluate afterschool activities and weekend commitments, keeping in mind that unstructured play and downtime are essential to your child's holistic development.

REFLECTIONS ⌇

While all these ideas may inspire you to reimagine a simpler home life, be sure not to let them become just another complicating expectation. For one mama, letting the marvelous mess of life animate her home may be the simplest option. For another, some careful trimming may banish her anxiety and allow her to breathe. No matter how you go about it, the underlying invitation is to KEEP IT SIMPLE, SWEETHEART!

SACRED MOTHERHOOD PRACTICE ⌇

REVIVE THE SABBATH. Across many religious and cultural traditions, the Sabbath is a day of rest and prayer. In this spirit, set aside a timeout for yourself each week (perhaps a Friday afternoon, Saturday, or Sunday) or once a month (possibly at the beginning of a new moon, or the start of your menstrual flow), dedicated to simplicity, relaxation, and spiritual practice. Begin and end your Sabbath with a simple ritual, and be intentional about what you invite into this sacred space.

IDEAS ⌇

- PUT AN END TO THE SHIT-SHUFFLE. Rid your home of excess stuff by removing all the items—broken toys, meaningless tzotchkes, dusty magazines—that no longer serve a purpose or enliven your soul. Then keep the chaos at bay with just fifteen minutes of decluttering at the end of each day.

- LET GO SO THAT YOU CAN KEEP UP. Liberate yourself and/or your children from one obligation or activity that does not add significantly to your quality of life. Remember that this will free up time and energy for the things you *do* love.

PAIRINGS ⌇

- Books: *The Life-Changing Magic of Tidying Up: The Japanese Art of Decluttering and Organizing* by Marie Kondo and *Simplicity Parenting: Using the Extraordinary Power of Less to Raise Calmer, Happier, and More Secure Kids* by Kim John Payne

journal on

Simplicity

How might you lessen the distraction of thoughts, activities, and things in order to welcome more *bliss*?

Patience

understanding right timing

The greatest prayer is patience.
—THE BUDDHA

The sun rises and sets every day, in concert with the rotation of the Earth. There is no rushing it; it just moves steadily, effortlessly, and with universal patience. Here on Earth, the bees can only make honey after the flowers have blossomed and are ready to share their glorious nectar. It's all about RIGHT TIMING, which unlocks the deep knowledge of patience, divinity, and trust.

As a mother, you had to grasp this wisdom quickly—and for real!—to birth your babies. But, as your children grow, patience can become an arduous spiritual practice, helping you discover the endurance and limit of your emotional strength. This week, we say a prayer for patience.

YOU ⟋◌⟍

Patience lives in understanding, and thrives on inner knowing. The more you practice compassion and cultivate self-knowledge, the higher your patience threshold tends to be. When you become a mother, life grows infinitely busier. The to-do list never ends!

In the midst of it all, how can you find time to be generous with yourself as you grow into motherhood? A lovely Zen adage says, "You should sit in meditation twenty minutes every day, unless you are too busy—if so, you should sit for an hour." Although this seems nearly impossible for most modern mamas, the saying speaks to the vital importance of making space to attune yourself with the infinite wisdom within you, so that you can truly be of service no matter what is happening.

While you work on finding time to sit in stillness, motherhood will offer up ample opportunities for you to exercise your patience. Many times you will fail to meet this challenge in the way you had intended. We *all* lose our patience sometimes! And that's okay. The principle of right timing teaches that you can only pick the fruit and enjoy its sweetness when it is ready—and that just depends upon the fruit.

Sometimes you must wait until the moment is ripe (or rotten!) to realize that you are now ready to welcome a new way of being.

YOUR SOUL ⌒〜

When the student is ready, the teacher will appear.
—BUDDHIST PROVERB

Patience is the ever-ready teacher that shows up when you need it most. If you lack patience, you are likely to be asked on many occasions to find it nonetheless. Maybe you have a baby who cries a lot and brings you to your edge, or perhaps you can't handle too much noise, or mess, or conflict.

Whatever it is that pushes your buttons, receive it as a gift that spurs you to learn and grow toward your highest self. When you have grasped this teaching, you will be presented new opportunities for growth. Welcome them all! Practice *inviting* patience into your mothering, and trust that you will only be given what you can truly handle.

YOUR CHILD ⌒〜

Raise your words, not your voice. It is rain that grows flowers, not thunder.
—RUMI

Like it or not, your children mirror your unresolved issues, so they have the unique ability to push the limits of your patience. There are times when I am at the crossroads of turning an insanely out-of-control situation into either a "teachable moment" or a "lose-my-shit moment." The cool thing is that I am finally at a spiritual place in my life where *I can choose!* I don't have to react to my kids' meltdowns with frustration or anger. I can choose to look beyond the situation that is tweaking me, and see very clearly the pain within my child in that moment.

Sacred Motherhood asks you to have patience with your child—but also with yourself. Do not cast a stone at yourself if you lose it from time to time. Take it as encouragement to learn, and to express yourself with greater compassion the next go-round. We are all human beings striving for happiness, peace, and love. Sometimes these aspirations get mired in our past wounds, and muck up the pure water we all want to drink. It's all okay—remember that!

REFLECTIONS ❧

As mothers, it can be especially hard to shake ourselves free of our failures because we desperately want to give our children the best we can possibly offer. Self-forgiveness can be easier when you trust RIGHT TIMING. In this case, "right timing" means that there is a reason for what you get—and when you get it, the trick is to see every moment, especially the hard ones, as holding exactly the experience or lesson that you need to continue walking your karmic path in life.

SACRED MOTHERHOOD PRACTICE ❧

PRACTICE PATIENCE. Invite patience into your life each day. Take a walk with your toddler. Chaperone your teenager's class trip. Realize that when you ask for patience, you will likely receive opportunities to *practice* it. Ask anyway! With further practice and greater patience, you will become more tranquil and open to perceiving all the gifts inside you.

IDEAS ❧

- PRAY FOR PATIENCE. Create a patience mantra—a short, positive saying such as "I am becoming patience." Use your mala (prayer beads) to help you practice your mantra throughout the day and infuse your being with patience.

- ADD A MUDRA. Mudras are sacred hand gestures. Use the *Lotus Mudra* to open yourself and receive patience: Put the lower edges of your hands together, palms facing each other but not touching. Next bring your two pinkies together. And then bring your two thumbs together. Keep your palms and other fingers spread open like a lotus flower in full bloom. Close your eyes and ask for patience, especially during trying moments.

pairings ⟳

· Crystal: Labradorite is associated with the heart chakra, and amplifies patience. Carry this crystal as a "touchstone" reminder of patient endurance in your mothering.
· Music: "Patience" by Redbird

journal on
Patience

Use this space to call in patience as a teacher. Reflect on what situations or behaviors test your patience. Describe how you might trust RIGHT TIMING, and respond with equanimity. Then create a patience mantra to support this vision—choose a few powerful, positive words that you can repeat to anchor your intention firmly inside yourself.

Tears + Fears

*mothering through
the emotions*

The Medicine Wheel teachings that have helped inspire and organize this book speak about summer in relationship to the waters of emotion. This week, with summer in full swing, we are calling a timeout for you to be present to the tears and fears of motherhood.

YOU ❧

Mothering engages the full catastrophe of human emotions—the extremes of everything from fathomless love to biting anger and paralyzing fear. The rapture and travails of motherhood deliver a whole new range of emotional experience, including countless tears of joy, frustration, and sadness. Yet no one prepares mothers for this ride, and many mamas are reluctant to talk about how they are feeling. What to do? *Get real.*

Start by sharing how you feel with your soul-sisters, if you have not done this already. And don't hide from your family. If you never saw your own mother cry, it may be harder for you to share your tears with others. Yet it is important for your partner and your children to see and love *all* of who you are.

Witnessing a smorgasbord of emotions in their mama also allows children to recognize and better understand the emotions moving through their own selves. Children learn by imitation, so if you can deal with your emotions through healthy expression rather than repression or transgression—neither stifling them nor acting them out thoughtlessly and inappropriately—you also lay a beautiful ground of wholeness for your child's future.

YOUR SOUL ❧

Opening yourself wholly to the gift of emotion means finding the courage to experience whatever you feel in a given moment. As an emotion begins to surface, do you let it move up and out of you, or do you attempt to block it? The image of a geyser comes to mind—if you opt for the blocking defense, probably because the feeling is overwhelming, scary, or unfamiliar, then the emotion builds up pressure inside you and will eventually erupt—or stagnate below the surface. If, instead of denying your emotion out of fear and judgment, you greet it with curiosity and compassion, it will flow through you like healing waters.

YOUR CHILD ℰ⟋

Some children have difficulty experiencing their emotions; others are deeply moved by waves of feeling. Navigating these waters with your children may or may not be smooth sailing. One child may trigger you more readily than the next, or you may find it difficult to relate to the emotions of your child due to his temperament or developmental stage. As you stretch to meet the inevitable challenges, let love buoy your learning. By turning this love toward yourself and accepting your own emotions, you can then extend a compassionate hand to your children when they are deluged by emotions.

The word compassion literally means to be with ("com-") the suffering or strong feelings ("passion") of others. So the compassionate response to your child's emotion is to simply *be with it.* Don't push it away, or even try to "fix" it. Rather, do your best to just be fully present with whatever is arising, no matter how uncomfortable it is for you. Be curious, and practice deep listening. Offer reassurance, especially in the form of hugs, or grant space if that's what's needed. And remember that your child (and many adults) won't always have the words to express what they are feeling, and may resort to acting out their emotions—which is not always pretty. Take heart, and stay with it.

REFLECTIONS ℰ⟋

Young children are extraordinary teachers about the nature of emotional energy. They do not yet know how to stifle their emotions, or cling to them. For these pure beings, anger simply arrives, emotes, and moves on, making room for the next wave. One moment they may be in tears, and giggling with delight the next. How can you respect this innate wisdom, and reclaim it for your own self?

SACRED MOTHERHOOD PRACTICE ❧

COMMIT TO LOVING YOURSELF AS AN EMOTIONAL BEING. This week, whenever you feel an emotion bubbling up, give yourself permission to feel it all the way to the depth of your being. Notice its layers. Anger may transform into sadness, then gratitude, and finally joy. Experience whatever emotion is present, without growing attached to it. Allow it to move like a wave, arising, changing, and ultimately disappearing back into the vast ocean of existence.

IDEAS ❧

- WHAT COLOR IS SADNESS? Help your children understand and express emotions by talking about them. Open the dialogue by naming your own emotions or inquiring about how they feel: "You threw that crayon. Are you frustrated?" Or get creative and invite your child to paint a picture of how it feels to be sad or happy, worried or angry.
- MAKE TIME FOR TEARS. When your child falls down—literally or figuratively—let the tears flow. Don't rush to quiet the storm or solve the problem. Just hold space, allowing your child to experience both vulnerability and resilience.

PAIRINGS ❧

- Book: *When Things Fall Apart: Heart Advice for Difficult Times* by Pema Chödrön
- Movie: *Inside Out* by Pixar Animation Studios
- Music: "I Am the Water" by Ardhana Silvermoon

Tears + Fears

When the emotional waters grow turbulent this week, sneak away to write. Tune into your body: What area is drawing your attention? How does it feel—tense, tingly, hot, or cold? Stay with the experience, and then describe what happens.

_____

_____

_____

_____

_____

_____

_____

_____

_____

_____

_____

_____

_____

Losing It

channeling your fire

Although it is rarely acknowledged, all mothers possess a breaking point. Some-
where on the way to the grocery store, between phone calls from teachers and
bickering in the back seat, even Mother Teresa herself would surely lose it some
days. We've all been there, and are ashamed to admit it, but in revealing the truth
we uncover compassion and stand the chance of charting a new course.

YOU ⟋

At the very mention of "losing it," most mamas probably feel the urge
to run—but stick around to encounter the nitty-grittiness of motherhood, and therein greet a new teacher. Motherhood brings unfath-
omable love and unprecedented joy, but it can also bring out your
demons like nothing else. Why is that?

To be sure, the daily annoyances and frustrations of mothering
can build up and trigger reactions that catch you by surprise. Add to
that sleep deprivation, worry, and lack of space to center yourself,
and it is a miracle that you keep it together as often as you do. But
sometimes you don't.

Learning to release and *channel your fire* so that you can speak and
act with dignity is one of the most valuable lessons of motherhood.
This takes practice. To begin, call up a healthy dose of compassion
for yourself. Suppressing or denying your exasperation and anger
only ensures that their flames will lick you or your beloveds when
you least expect it. Instead of trying to force yourself to behave—or
igniting an inferno—make friends with your ire. Approach it with
understanding, and a curiosity to find out what message it carries
for you.

YOUR SOUL ⟋

When you treat losing it as a fiery aperture that lets you see into yourself, you can gain insight and invite transformation. For many of us,
our most vulnerable emotions and toughest defenses were picked
up during childhood. It's no wonder that our children unwittingly
awaken the old demons in us that are ready to be discharged.

Learning to honor your fire as a teacher and owning its intense light in the name of change, creation, and protection is a gradual process. Be brave, be patient, and ask for help. Identify on which occasions you are most likely to become hot-headed. What tools do you have to pull yourself back from that edge and wait for the blaze to die down? How can you approach those tense times in a different way, so that you are less likely to combust? When you do lose it, how can you tend to the burn victims? Acknowledgment, apology, and forgiveness can create a powerful healing salve for yourself and others.

YOUR CHILD ❧

From tantrums to tears, children are no strangers to the experience of losing their cool. The beauty of this is that they have not yet become attached to these intense emotions, but simply ride their waves as pure energy, allowing them to disperse and transmute. As a mother, you can resist and attempt to control these cycles—or you can honor them as you are learning to do for yourself.

Try befriending your child's anger and frustration. Be curious about what might be sparking these emotions: Does your child feel small, insecure, or afraid? What can you do to make things less difficult? It might help to consider how your own inner child would like to be cared for when she is feeling out of control.

REFLECTIONS ❧

In a calm moment, take a look at the illusions and unconscious beliefs that are chaining you to your raw emotions. Perhaps, like me, you fear that you will not be loved if you are not perfect—but, alas! Perfection is an insane-making pursuit in motherhood. Or perhaps you are confusing rage with strength. Look deep to see if you can free the energy you have tied to your temper, and reclaim it as a creative force.

SACRED MOTHERHOOD PRACTICE ❧

CALL UPON YOUR PLANT ALLIES. When you feel yourself getting wound up, light a smudge-stick of sage or cedar to clear the air. Let the sacred healing smoke wash over you, and then waft it around your home to dispel any lingering negativity. You can also smudge to cleanse your mind, body, and spirit at the start or end of each day.

IDEAS

- COME OUT OF THE CLOSET. Share with your partner or a close friend about your breaking point, and ask for support. Your shadow has the most power when you try to keep it in the dark. Let there be light!

- CREATE A "PEACE TENT" IN YOUR HOME. This is a sacred place where you or your children can retreat when you feel your temper rising. Make it beautiful, inviting, and calming. A bottle of Rescue Remedy, a box of tissues, some healing stones, and a soft place to land are a few of the necessary accoutrements. Then model for your children how and when to *use it before you lose it.*

PAIRINGS

- Crystal: Carnelian is an ideal stone to carry or wear to help deal with intense emotions without reacting. It helps to balance the inner self and call in the support of your spirit guides.

- Music: "Thunder" by Leona Lewis

Losing It

What is your relationship to rage? What is your fire asking you to transform? And when is it okay to be fierce and let your she-bear rip?

_____

_____

_____

_____

_____

_____

_____

_____

_____

_____

_____

_____

_____

_____

_____

_____

Body As Temple

embracing self-love

Our Earth Mother is the body that supports every living being. She is fertile, round, and whole. She gives of herself freely, abundantly, and without judgment.

You too give beyond measure, caring for others all day long with little or no break. When was the last time you paused to fully appreciate your body, and everything it allows you to do? This week is all about making time to love and honor your mothering body as a SACRED TEMPLE.

YOU ॰

Your body is your temple. Keep it pure and clean for the soul to reside in.
—B.K.S. IYENGAR

Women are fed millions of messages about our bodies. We're told over and over again what we should look like, and what the standard of beauty is for our appearance. But a mother's body is shaped differently than a supermodel's body. Your body is likely to have changed since you were a maiden! As a mother, you have been beautifully sculpted by nature to have fuller hips that can birth and carry the babes, larger breasts that fill with mama's milk to feed young ones, and even a softer belly for children to lie on.

How do you feel about your body, now that you are a mother? Do you see yourself as the goddess that you are? Do you treat your body as a temple? What do you feed your body, and your body image?

Feeding negativity to your body is just as dangerous as taking in toxins like tobacco smoke, drugs, processed foods, and excess sugar. And if you have a poor body image, your children will pick up those vibrations even if you don't express them out loud. You want your children to grow up feeling good about themselves, which means you need to work on transforming any negative thoughts you may have about your own body into positive, *self-loving* messages.

YOUR SOUL ॰

To love and honor your body is to love and honor the *divine*. Every body is a physical manifestation of spirit, and how you have shown up in this world is your personal expression of beauty. When you are focused on caring for others, it is easy to forget that your body is a holy vessel in service to your soul's work.

Making space for self-love and regular care routines brings the focus back to your physical well-being. Maybe you can set aside time for a weekly massage, a short catnap, a daily yoga practice, or a walk in nature to connect inward as well as exercise. And you definitely want to ensure that your body-temple is given whole, fresh foods that will nourish it, keeping you vital and strong for the joys and labors of motherhood

Get on it, girl! Love up your body. It is the sacred house of *you!*

YOUR CHILD ❧

Children are the world's best mimics. Whatever you model for your children, they will incorporate into their lives and beings. This is precisely why it's critical for you to be physically and spiritually healthy. How you treat your body will directly affect the way your own children treat their bodies.

Seen this way, motherhood is just huge! We have to guide these little beings the best we can, and sometimes that means *we* must change our own bad habits and negative self-talk, so that we don't pass them on to our children. Instead, we can teach them what is good and healthy for their bodies, by feeding our own bodies well, or demonstrating (by doing it ourselves!) how important it is to go outside and move our bodies each day. Then they will not only feel better inside, they will be living in high vibration without even trying.

REFLECTIONS ❧

When you were growing up, what messages did you receive about how your body should look, and be treated? What were you taught about food? These are deep questions that, once answered, can help you shift onto a better path. In particular, look at how you treat your body in times of stress, when you are most likely to fall back on childhood patterns and feelings.

SACRED MOTHERHOOD PRACTICE ⌒

TREAT YOUR BODY TO A DAILY LOVEFEST. Commit to treating your body like a temple by creating a self-love practice that will help sustain you throughout your mothering years and beyond. No matter what form it takes—walking, bubble baths, whole foods, yoga, sex—this will help you put the concept of honoring your body into practice.

IDEAS ⌒

- ADORN YOUR SACRED BODY. Choose clothing that feels comfortable, sexy, beautiful, and *divine!* Risk a little fashion adventure, if you've become stuck in a wardrobe rut. Feel *big love* for your body, and then wear it on your sleeve.

- ANOINT YOUR BODY. Create a BODY-AS-TEMPLE OIL—and anoint yourself!

BODY-AS-TEMPLE OIL

Note: You can purchase these essences at a local health food store or online.

> 2 oz. sweet almond or coconut oil
>
> 10 drops Orchid Queen Flower Essence (this Quan Yin of essences connects you with your inner divinity)
>
> 10 drops Magnolia Flower Essence (for clearing, purifying, and raising you to your highest vibration)
>
> 10 drops ylang-ylang essential oil
>
> 5 drops cedar or patchouli essential oil
>
> 7 drops bergamot or mandarin (orange) essential oil

Mix all ingredients in a small, beautiful jar. Warm gently before applying this oil to your body as a sacred offering to self.

PAIRINGS ⌒

- Music: "Video" by India Arie, and "Try" by Colbie Caillat
- Book: *Beautiful Girl: Celebrating the Wonders of Your Body* by Christiane Northrup and Kristina Tracy

journal on

Body as Temple

Write about what BODY AS TEMPLE means to YOU, and then create a fitting SELF-LOVE action plan.

_____

_____

_____

_____

_____

_____

_____

_____

_____

_____

_____

_____

_____

_____

_____

_____

_____

Sacred Relationship

keeping the love alive

I crave a love so deep that the ocean would be jealous.
—ANONYMOUS

Like the dawning of a bright summer morning, the sun rises on a new day of joy and possibility in love. If you are currently in a relationship, read this chapter deeply, and hang on every word, because it will help you! If you are not currently in a relationship, read this chapter even more ferociously, as this vision can help you call in the one who will respond to your body, mind, and spirit in a way that you may never have experienced yet. But before you read further, ask yourself this question: "Do I believe in love?"

YOU ⸱⸱

I once had a thousand desires, but in my one desire to know you, all else melted away.
—RUMI

Love knocks at your door, charming you to open up and invite it into your life. There is no room for fear in SACRED LOVE, only the understanding that love brings with it the illumination of a heart-path that you'll be fortunate to walk, if you are courageous.

As you set off down the sacred path of love, one of the most damaging and pervasive myths in our culture, perpetuated by movies, books, and TV, is that when you meet the "right" person, you will fall in love and live "happily ever after." Love in real life is a complex feeling, serving up a buffet of heart nourishment including *eros* (sensuality and passion), *philia* (the love between friends), *agape* (spiritual love; a willingness to live in compassion), and *divinity* (the higher path of understanding that we are *one* reflection of the divine in each other).

Anyone who has ever fallen in love can tell you that the intense initial phase of love will fade over time. In the beginning, when physical attraction is potent, the sense of desire can be almost overwhelming, and *everything* about your beloved seems wonderful. During this "obsessive love" stage, you feel good, so you naturally express only positive, loving thoughts. The purpose of this phase in a relationship is essentially the "cupid effect," in which two people who share a destiny are thrown together with a powerful attractive force. But since this only starts the ball rolling, where the relationship goes from there is up to the couple.

Everyone has heard that relationships take work. It is true that relationships call for conscious choices, requiring us to take actions that support and strengthen the relationship while refraining from other actions that weaken and damage it. This heart-work stage of "intentional love" is a more mature love, and looks very different from obsessive love. It brings deeper joy and fulfillment than the initial love spell can ever produce.

When you add children into any relationship, everything changes. Tag-teaming, lack of sleep, changing roles, and little time for intimacy can break down the strongest connection between partners. The good news is that committed relationship practices, open communication, and support from other couples can help you meet even these challenges—and thrive!

YOUR SOUL ⌒〜⊃

With or without children, heart-work is not easy. Creating a sacred relationship takes profound commitment and strength. It also takes endless forgiveness, and the warrior spirit of perseverance and dedication.

In the beginning, you may find yourself doubting that you or your relationship can change. YES, change is possible! With every act of love and giving, with every gesture of forgiveness and openness, and with every moment spent loving your beloved, you *are* changing. As with anything, sometimes it is hard to see any immediate changes, and other times you progress miles in the snap of a finger. So if you are ready (and you are, or you wouldn't be reading this right now!), do not wait another moment to embark on your journey towards a more sacred relationship full of romance, passion, and deep connection.

YOUR CHILD ⌒

Sacred relationship work not only benefits you and your beloved, it deeply affects the whole family. Your children observe you every single day, and develop all of their expectations, hopes, and dreams for love based on what they see, hear, and experience. This means you are the one teaching them how to *do love*.

Do you and your love kiss in front of the children? Do you laugh, and are you playful with each other? Do you do silly, sweet romantic things for each other? Do you still feel sexually attracted to each other? Do you share a quality of love that you want your children to witness every day?

Or do you get lost in so many daily tasks that you have become more like roommates? Do you argue more often than you speak from the heart? Answer these questions with fierce honesty so that you can fire up your heart-work and create a sacred relationship that will inspire your children to seek love's many gifts when they become adults.

REFLECTIONS ⌒

Spend some time reflecting on the quality of the relationship you have with your beloved since beginning your family. If your relationship is not where you want it to be, you can make it better! Even if your relationship is in a great, connected place, you can always elevate it to an even higher vibration. Above all, commit to *do no harm!* This is the first and only real rule in love.

SACRED MOTHERHOOD PRACTICE ⌒

CREATE A SACRED RELATIONSHIP. Use these Sacred Relationship practices with your beloved *daily* to feed your intentional love and deep connection!

· Each and every time you enter and leave your beloved's presence, give him or her a hug and a kiss, and say, "You are my love." Make it a real hug, and a kiss on the lips, and look into their eyes when you remind your beloved—and yourself—that this person is your truest love.

- At some time during the day, say something positive about your beloved to another person.

- Each day, leave at least one note with romantic or complimentary love words, in a place where your beloved will find it.

- From this day forward, whenever you address your partner, refer to him or her as your "BELOVED." This is a sacred term!

- Slow-dance at least once a week!

- Sacred Kiss! Sit facing each other, and kiss and make out for the length of one song.

- NAKED TIME! Take fifteen minutes of every single day to just lie naked with your beloved. This is not about sex; it is just about removing any and all barriers between you so that you can be reminded in your physical bodies of the spiritual connection you two share, and how divine that connection truly is. Try this especially in times of anger; it can powerfully take you to a very different level of relating.

IDEAS ❧

- PRACTICE HEART-TO-HEART MEDITATION. Choose a romantic song that the two of you like, and sit facing each other with your knees touching. Then place your right hand on one another's hearts, and use your left hand to cover the partner's hand on your own chest. Look deeply into each other's eyes, and open to your beloved for the length of the song. Maintain your gaze even if it gets uncomfortable. As you experience your love flowing back and forth, recall the emotions from your first date. Reflect on where you went, what you said, what you wore, and how you felt. Just enjoy these memories, and your heart-to-heart connection.

- ATTEND A SACRED RELATIONSHIP LIVE RETREAT. If you believe that your relationship needs more work, or you just want to learn how to elevate it to a sacred level, then come to a Sacred Relationship Live Retreat. They are held all over the world, and are run by Tim and Anni Daulter. (Check our website for more details: www.oursacred relationship.com.)

pairings ❧

- Book: *The Five Love Languages: How to Express Heartfelt Commitment to Your Mate* by Gary Chapman

- Music: "One and Only" by Adele, and "Kiss Me" and "Thinking Out Loud" by Ed Sheeran

journal on

Sacred Relationship

This week, use your journal space to reflect on your relationship by answering the following questions. Ask your beloved to respond to them as well, and then spend time discussing the answers you both gave.

SACRED RELATIONSHIP "Taking Stock" Questionnaire:

· My biggest complaint about my relationship is …

· I feel that my beloved is loving towards me when he/she …

· My beloved feels loved by me when I …

· I feel that my beloved is hurtful towards me when he/she …

· My beloved feels hurt by me when I …

· My beloved's most loving act of service toward me was …

· My beloved's most hurtful act that still lives in me was when …

· What portion of my time do I spend in positive thoughts and feelings about my beloved (___% positive)? How much time do I give to negative thoughts and feelings (___% negative)?

· How many hours per week do I spend connecting deeply on a physical and emotional level with my beloved? (Shared experiences, such as watching a movie or sleeping next to each other, do not count!)

Earth

Abundance

Dreaming

Pumpkins

Mystery

Maple Leaves

Intuition

Shadow

Forgiveness

Rites of Passage

Soul

Hibernation

I AM

Magic

Wisdom

Cinnamon

Healing

Harvest

Remembrance

Walking Your Path

trust in your way

Every path, every street in the world, is your walking meditation.
—THICH NHAT HANH

The seasons of motherhood are as varied as Mother Nature's beauty, and quite as vast. With fall comes a stillness and inwardness, balancing the expansive energy of summer. The invitation this week, as we turn to greet a new season, is to stop and seek your own TRUTH.

One of the scariest dragons a mother must slay is her own self-doubt. Becoming a mother does not mean you magically have all the answers to life—in fact, it means quite the opposite! You are now filled with enough questions to fill a library, and you likely have access to infinite books and people wanting to sway you in a particular direction. This avalanche of helpful information can topple you over and paralyze you with uncertainty. To find your way through it all, you must TRUST the path you have chosen.

YOU ☙

Putting one foot in front of the other every single day is the only way to do motherhood. You can read every single parenting book, get advice from every expert and every person who *thinks* she is an expert, and still be left wondering. Doubt haunts you. It keeps you questioning whether you did right or wrong by your child. You want so badly to do everything *right*—but whose standards are you living by, anyway?

Let's say, for example, that you want your new baby or older child (or both) to sleep in your bed with you, but your mother-in-law thinks that is absolutely the wrong thing to do. What do you do? You consider yourself a conscious mom, and in an attempt to gather all the information, you look to those around you for guidance. However, something in your gut just tells you that what you want to do is the right thing for your family. Can you stand in your own power and walk your path as you see fit? Can you meet naysayers with a *strong back* and an *open heart*?

YOUR SOUL ❧

Motherhood catapults you into both wisdom and inexperience—in the same moment—multiple times a day. With this paradox as your compass, how do you absolutely know which way to go? The answer is that you don't. Instead, you TRUST, and you understand that you and your child signed up to navigate this lifetime together. Sharing your inner gold and wealth of personal experience with this child is part of what you are meant to do in this lifetime. And there is special knowledge that only you have about this particular child to help her on her karmic journey. This is a *sacred* relationship that the two of you have, and it can only be nurtured one way—*your way*.

This does not mean that you stop seeking information and experiences to help you grow, stay inspired, and explore new territory; you continue doing this, but always come back to trusting your way and walking the path that *only you* can walk. You will recognize your path when you come upon it, because it will whisper only your name.

YOUR CHILD ❧

The path of childhood is filled with wonder and magic, but there are also roots to trip over, and scary noises in the bushes. There is no telling what your child may encounter on her destined path, and while you can guide her along, you cannot walk it for her. This can be a bitter bite of reality for us mamas, because we don't want our little ones to ever face a demon on their journeys through life.

No mother wants to see her children suffer in any way—and yet sometimes they do. This can leave you feeling wounded, and powerless. While there is so much beyond your control, you can reframe how you experience challenging situations by replacing powerlessness with a DEEP TRUST that whatever is happening is one of the lessons your child came into this world to learn. Your role is to hold loving space and provide wise counsel as your child unfolds his or her own dharma.

REFLECTIONS ⌒

When you are sitting in a *rooted* place of deep trust, you can better attune to what is unfolding, moment-to-moment. You can step out of your habitual responses to your children's constantly changing needs. And you can navigate the unmapped terrain of motherhood with more joy and less fear.

SACRED MOTHERHOOD PRACTICE ⌒

LIGHT A CANDLE FOR YOUR SACRED PATH. Every morning, light a candle to honor your way through that day. Set an intention of seeking to be your best self for the day and trusting yourself to navigate the myriad of daily tribulations that may unfold. Say a pray for GRACE and EASE on your path of motherhood.

IDEAS ⌒

- SLEEP ON IT. When you have a problem that you cannot solve, or a situation that confounds you, gather any information and guidance that you feel may help, and then sleep on it. For three nights, ask for insight before drifting off to sleep. When you wake, write down the first thing that comes to mind, whether it is a dream image or a clear action plan. Then trust that what is arising from deep within you is *your way* forward.

- OPEN TO WISDOM FROM THE MOUTHS OF BABES. Take time to listen to your child when challenges arise and you cannot see the forest for the trees. Often children are not as attached to outcomes as adults, and can more clearly name the pathway that is unfolding. In particular, be sure to consult your child when the situation pertains to them, if they are old enough to weigh the options. For example, if you are having a hard time deciding which school your child should attend—ask your child!

pairings ❧

- Book: *Native Spirit Oracle Cards: A 44-Card Deck and Guidebook* by Denise Linn
- Crystal: Amazonite is a centering stone that can help to keep you on your path amidst the chaos and confusion of motherhood. It is also a powerful stone of protection that can keep undesirable energies and influences out of your life. Amazon women are said to have used it in their shields!
- Movie: *Brave* by Pixar Animation Studios
- Music: "Brave" by Sara Bareilles

journal on

Walking Your Path

Spend time journaling about your
motherhood journey, and all of the
twists and turns that have unfolded
along the way. How have you trusted
yourself? How have you trusted
your path?

Intuition

the wisdom within

As temperatures drop and the heightened energy of summer wanes, fall is the season to turn inward. Come indoors and take stock of your family life. Then look deep inside to rediscover the Wise Woman within you.

YOU ⟡

Intuition is a hallmark of motherhood. Exercise this superpower to discern how best to support your child, or to course-correct your journey as a mother. When you are willing to heed the warnings of your SIXTH SENSE, you can also perceive when things are off-kilter.

You might sniff out a lie, or follow a hunch to avoid danger; but even with a mother's illustrious intuition, the cacophony of expert advice and conflicting opinions can drown out the voice of your inner knowing. From the latest parenting bible to the lady at the checkout stand, everyone seems to know (and to want to tell you!) how you should raise your children. Do you know how? Of course! Trust that you know, deep down, what is best for you and yours.

As you listen to the wisdom within, notice where and when doubt surfaces. Are you thrown off by your mother's comments? Or does everything seem peachy until you get up to pee in the night and then begin to fret? This week, make a commitment to check yourself when you begin to spin into self-doubt. Return to your center. Practice staying true to your deeper knowing even if it surprises you, or diverges from your "grand plan."

YOUR SOUL ⟡

In fall, everything—leaves, seeds, and summer fruits—nestle down into the earth to break down, return their essence, and feed new life. It is also time for you to go within and reconnect to your innermost gifts. Sometimes you need nothing more than a cozy nook and your journal to lead you inward. Other times, the outward expansion of motherhood takes you so far from your deeper self that this takes several days of holing up like a bear. This week, do whatever it takes to come home to *you.*

When you do, you may notice that the hum of your inherent knowing has grown faint. From time to time, every mama needs a little help reviving her voice of wisdom. In addition to yoga, meditation, dreaming, and other awareness-raising practices, inspiration decks can summon the higher spiritual knowledge inside you. Turn to *The Mother's Wisdom Deck,* the first inspiration deck devoted to the spiritual journey of motherhood (see "Pairings" in Week 1). The deck's fifty-two cards mirror both sacred and mundane aspects of mothering, and serve as a doorway to access your intuitive, inner knowing in the throes of the everyday.

YOUR CHILD ❧

The good news is that children are far more intuitive than most adults. They are *highly sensitive,* and have not yet learned to filter their perceptions. As you re-up your relationship with the Wise Woman within, also honor and uphold this inborn gift in your child. Whenever you get the chance, affirm the messages he receives through his sixth sense.

If your child tells you that something feels either wrong or right-on, take him seriously, and take time to help him understand how he is sourcing this information. Ask him whether he is feeling something in his gut. Or help him to recognize when he is following a sense of elation and ease. Also, give him opportunities whenever possible to make choices from this seat of wisdom. One mama I admire invites her son to pick a homeopathic remedy whenever he is sick, and marvels at his sagacious selections. Indeed, the vast knowing within these small beings never ceases to amaze!

REFLECTIONS ❧

As adults, we tend to think that we know more than children, and therefore they should listen to us. While this may be true in some ways, in other ways it is way off-base. Children come into this world with a Beginner's Mind, and a deep desire to understand the inner and outer worlds. We adults often kick this attitude to the curb, replacing it with a know-it-all mindset. What we need to understand is that Beginner's Mind is the only place from which we can forever seek the WISDOM WITHIN.

SACRED MOTHERHOOD PRACTICE ℰ🙰

CALL FORTH THE WISDOM WITHIN. Draw a card from your favorite divination or inspiration deck each day. Start by centering yourself, and light a candle. Next, shuffle the deck while asking for guidance—pose a question, ponder a problem, or simply hold the intention to serve the greatest good. Place your deck face down, and fan the cards out in front of you. Close your eyes, allowing your hand and soul to pick a card. Then contemplate the card, and receive its messages through its imagery and words. Keep your mind open, trust your interpretation, and give yourself full permission to call forth the wisdom within *you*.

IDEAS ℰ🙰

- OPEN YOUR THIRD EYE. Create an Inner-Knowing Oil to anoint your third eye—the seat of your higher perception—as you call up the powers of your intuition

- FOSTER INTUITION. When you and your child arrive at a new place, or meet a new person, take a moment to check in with your child. Inquire how he feels about the space or individual. Listen openly, and validate his intuitive hit. Have fun comparing notes and following hunches.

INNER-KNOWING OIL

3 drops lotus flower essence

4 drops labradorite essence

5 drops sweet orange essential oil

5 drops sandalwood essential oil

Fill a one-ounce rollerball-top container almost full with Rose Oil (see "Ideas" in Week 2) and mix the above ingredients into it.

pairings ⌒

· Color: Indigo is the color of the spirit world. Use this color to tap your inner knowing, by painting some pages in your journal with an indigo blue, and asking the universe to guide you to your wisdom within.

· Crystal: Amethyst enhances intuition by opening the third eye to perceive and understand what is happening in both the physical and spiritual worlds.

journal on
Intuition

Sometimes heeding the voice of
your intuition requires asking your
judging mind to pipe down! For
this exercise, we invite you to set a
timer for ten minutes, and commit to keeping your pen moving the
entire time—no pausing, no editing—only pure flow from the inside
out. When you are ready, respond to the following prompt: THE WISE
WOMAN WITHIN KNOWS ...

_____

_____

_____

_____

_____

_____

_____

_____

_____

_____

_____

_____

_____

Soulmates

the light in me sees
the light in you

Lovers don't finally meet somewhere. They're in each other all along.
—RUMI

Autumn is the season of the SOUL. *Having tuned inward last week, we now seek to understand how your soul's path intertwines with the path of your* SOULMATE. *There are many theories as to how we find our beloved partners in life, but the truth seems to lie in the lap of mystery and magic. In the summer, we looked at creating a sacred relationship with your beloved, to help build a solid foundation for long-lasting love. This week, we fall into the juicy nectar that pulled you to-gether for a shared destiny that only your two souls can fulfill.*

YOU ⌒

It was not into my ear that you whispered, but into my heart. It was not my lips you kissed, but my soul.
—JUDY GARLAND

Close your eyes, and remember the very first moment you saw your beloved. Let that delicate time ruminate inside of you. Whether you talked or giggled or exchanged phone numbers doesn't matter; what matters is that there was an energy exchange between you—something that whispered into your heart and kissed your soul. How your relationship formed and took on a life over time is your unique love story, but your soul recognizing the soul of another and saying YES is the essence of love between soulmates.

Soul recognition is a powerful force. It stirs feelings of invincibility and happiness within you, and lands a smile on your face from ear to ear. You act goofy and giddy, and feel butterflies in your stomach whenever your beloved's name is mentioned. I am convinced that soulmate love is born from superhero dust mixed with magic and mystery, and topped off with dark, oozing, delicious chocolate.

Why does this matter? Because you and your beloved share a SOUL CONTRACT that needs to be played out for the greater good of all.

The karma between you will reveal itself as your life together unfolds. But part of your destiny together has already manifested beauty, if you have brought a child into the world.

YOUR SOUL ⌒◡

Living out a karmic path with another person—even your greatest love if you are so blessed—can also be a challenge, and an ongoing teaching. Your soulmate can call up some of your most difficult lessons in this life, as part of the soul contract you share.

Sometimes your soulmate reflects your shadow and triggers your wounds, and although this may be painful, it can help you see places within yourself that need light, growth, or healing. It's also important for you to understand that, although you may not be together forever, you will be together until the dance you are meant to do together is done. This could take a whole lifetime (or many lifetimes), or it could be a short stint in the realm of Earthly love.

Regardless of the ups and downs and the number of years together, your relationship with your beloved is valuable in ways you may never fully grasp. You can be assured that it is part of your deepest soul-work in this lifetime. Your mind may play tricks on you, but your heart knows where it is supposed to be. To stay in the flow of love and life, *always* follow your heart.

YOUR CHILD ⌒◡

Your children also have soul contracts with you, and with your beloved. Their souls were destined to arrive in this world, at this time, with you as their mother. Quite likely, they were meant to enter through you and your beloved, and would not have been born at all if you hadn't come together. And if they needed to come into this life and into your arms through adoption, surrogacy, or any other blessed pathway, there was a soul conspiracy at play to bring you *all* together as family. Even if you are currently seeking a soulmate to partner with you in family life, you can bet that your soul *and* your child's soul are calling in that special someone together, if it is meant to be.

REFLECTIONS ⌒

Some folks may say that believing in true love and shared destinies is just for silly romantics—but isn't the possibility of sharing your life with other beautiful souls worth risking a little enlightened foolishness? Teach your child to believe in ooey-gooey love! Show your child how much you love each other by kissing and hugging in front of them, and making small romantic gestures that teach the languages of love. It's mind-blowing, *sacred* juju, when you think about it!

SACRED MOTHERHOOD PRACTICE ⌒

MAKE A LOVER'S FLOWER MANDALA. A mandala is a circular spiritual image that represents the whole universe—complete with cosmic connections and the impermanence of life—in one Beauty-Way circle. You can create your own to honor your sacred love.

Gather handfuls of flowers, leaves, and branches from your yard. Then sit with your beloved and co-create a Lover's Flower Mandala on the ground, arranging the items in a circular pattern, however it pleases you. As you work, share versions of your love story.

When you are finished, sweep up your flower creation and send the petals off into the wind, with a mutual prayer for your love to flourish in beauty and light.

IDEAS ⌒

- UNPLUG, AND PAY ATTENTION. Spend time with your beloved every night, unplugged from electronics and without distractions. Even for just fifteen minutes, give each other your undivided attention, and talk about what is meaningful to you and what is stirring in your souls.

- RAISE YOUR VIBRATION. Do this meditation with your soulmate to cleanse your energetic bodies and raise the level of your vibration, enhancing the connection between you: Sit next to your beloved, upright in a comfortable position. Close your eyes, and bring your attention to your breath. Once you feel relaxed and comfortable, visualize a bright white light at the base of your spine. As you breathe out, visualize the light beginning to rise up your spine, filling your body with white light. As you breathe in, visualize the light getting stronger and brighter. Then, on the next out-breath, see the light rising farther up your spine, filling you with white light. When the light reaches the top of your head, visualize it bursting through your head and shining up into the heavens, connecting you with your source and your beloved.

pairings ☙

- Book: *Universal Love Healing Oracle Cards* by Toni Carmine Salerno
- Music: "How Long Will I Love You" by Ellie Goulding, "My Love" by Jess Glynne, and "Sweet Love of Mine" by Joy Williams

Soulmates

Take a walk down memory lane, and write down the story of how you came together with your soulmate. Then take some time to reflect on where you are in your relationship now: Do you still share a deep connection? Do you feel you are with the right person? Is your relationship functioning at its highest possible vibration?

Nest

weaving a sacred home

The ache for home lives in all of us—the safe place where we can go as we are and not be questioned.

—MAYA ANGELOU

As the days grow shorter and the weather turns cooler, our innate impulse to ready the nest for winter begins to stir. Now is an ideal time to turn your attention toward HOME. *Our homes are where we experience safety and belonging, where we can relax into feeling held and accepted. Creating a sacred environment in which the soul can feel at home is a gift to you and your family. Just as a nest is woven of many fibers, your home is created from many threads. From playing with colors and textures to displaying objects and seeding memories, nesting is not just for the birds!*

YOU ᐧᐧ

Whether you're a stay-at-home mom or a working mom, whether you rent or own, and whether you plant deep roots or tend toward a nomadic life, your current abode is home base for your mothering.

Look around: What kind of home have you created? Do you adore your home, or would you rather swap it for a solitary cabin in the woods, or perhaps a penthouse in the city? Does it feel like an extension of you, with all your endearing quirks and flair? At the end of a long day, does your whole family (even the teenager!) gratefully land in the *welcoming embrace* of your home?

If so, right on! You have a knack for homemaking, and fall is the perfect opportunity to indulge (or develop) this gift by wrangling dust bunnies, rearranging treasures, and adorning the beautiful space that you have manifested.

If, on the other hand, you have yet to settle in a place that feels like home, spend this week realizing that you can remake your space by tending to even one small corner. Set your sights on creating a cozy nook with blankets, pillows, and special objects, along with a collection of favorite books. Make a point to nestle there with your children, and see if the BELONGING you have been seeking begins to appear.

YOUR SOUL ⟳

Going beneath the surface, the state of your home can serve as a barometer of your soul's well-being. If your home feels lived-in and comfortable, chances are that your whole being is grounded in contentment. If, instead, you have a "perfect" home that does not tolerate spills and scuffs, consider that you may be trying to control and avert life rather than accept and engage it. Or, on the other end of the spectrum, if your home has accumulated too much clutter, perhaps it is burying the clarity and simplicity you are craving.

At the end of the day, no matter what your personal style, if you have surrounded yourself and your family with *beauty,* you can be assured that your soul has been treated to a faithful mirror of its own radiance.

YOUR CHILD ⟳

For many people, early childhood memories are linked to places— the scary spare bedroom in Grandma's house, the little cabinet in the kitchen that was a good hiding spot, or the front stoop where you played house. It is not uncommon for adults to remember their childhood home in elaborate detail. I recall the color, pattern, and exact placement of the couch I would rest on when I came home from kindergarten. Whether the couch was from Saks or Sears, what matters is how it felt—soft and secure. In crafting our homes with care, we can help shape these warm and tender recollections for our children, and offer them happy associations with home, no matter where life may take them.

REFLECTIONS ⟳

As you sit in the comfort (or discomfort) of your home, tune into what "home" means to you. Recall the role that your childhood home played in your young life: Was it a place that you were drawn to, or that you wished to escape? What memories does it evoke? Remembering all the different places you have called home, which one stands out as your favorite? What do you love most about it? As you sift through the layers of your past homes, imagine what kind of space might reflect who you have become and where you now belong with your family.

SACRED MOTHERHOOD PRACTICE ⌾

MAKE A FAMILY HOME ALTAR. With your children, create and maintain a home altar to anchor the center of your home. Include special items that symbolize your family. Add flowers, candles, and offerings.

IDEAS ⌾

- CURATE YOUR HOME. Take time to go through your home, room by room, and evaluate your belongings. You don't have to do this all at once—just when the spirit moves you. Then hold onto only what you find meaningful, delightful, or absolutely necessary. Donate or recycle everything else. The empty space you create will give you a refreshing infusion of energy and expansiveness. Find special ways to display the objects that you have kept, to fully appreciate their beauty and/or utility.

- REVAMP YOUR CHILDREN'S ROOMS. Invite your children to refashion their bedrooms to express who they are. Help them identify what is special to them, and what they are ready to pass along. Create spaces for them to display words, images, and colors that express their interests and individuality.

PAIRINGS ⌾

- Book: *Handmade Home* by Mark and Sally Bailey
- Music: "Home" by Edward Sharpe and The Magnetic Zeros

journal on
Nest

Describe in detail the home you desire for you and your family. What does it look like? How does it feel? What are three things you can do this week to manifest a "home-coming"?

Nourish

*feeding your family
with love*

As we begin the slow descent into the darker months, the harvest season calls us back to the hearth, where family comes together around food. It is the time of year for scents of pumpkin-pie spice and cinnamon wafting around and warming hearts, for candlelit dinners shared with blessings of gratitude and love, and for the well-being that comes from sharing nourishing soups and just being with those dear to you. This week, we mix food with love and laughter to understand how nourishing others is one of motherhood's highest callings.

YOU ⌾⌣

What does it mean to NOURISH your family? In sacred-speak, to nourish is to *live by your heart*. Your love is the main ingredient in every recipe for your family's care; it contains healing, heart-warming, and life-giving magic. You hold the spoon that stirs the pot of nourishment you serve to your family every day. How and what you feed your family matters! The recipe is not the way; the way is the recipe.

I learned how to cook at the Tassajara Zen Mountain Center in Carmel Valley. They taught me the art of conscious community cooking, where each person is responsible for one ingredient or task. You have to put your full love and attention into your part of the meal, whether chopping tomatoes, washing lettuce leaves, or cooking rice. Every contribution is held as sacred.

When we bring this practice into our homes, channeling our presence and full awareness into cooking for our families and giving our children special jobs in the kitchen, we end up creating meals that are flavored with love—meals that nourish the body and feed the soul.

YOUR SOUL ⌾⌣

Food has a soul, and a story. Living in a hurried world, it's easy to forget this, and to overlook *how* you nourish yourself and others. Try taking the time to get to know each ingredient as if it were the richest color of paint you could use to complete a masterpiece. And respect the *prana* of food; its life-force has a purpose. Don't squander it!

Instead, play lovely music while you cook, to amplify the vibrational medicine of the food you eat and serve to your loved ones.

FOOD IS MEDICINE. If you forget all else, do not forget that! Our bodies either thrive or shut down, based on what we put into them. If you view the body as a temple, then cooking becomes a spiritual practice. Putting prayers into the food you are preparing; placing a healing crystal at the bottom of a pot of homemade soup; dancing, singing, and laughing in the kitchen—all of these can add to the medicine of your meals, and enhance the overall quality of *sacred nourishment* you are offering to your family.

YOUR CHILD ⌒

If you want to deeply nourish your family, invite your children into the kitchen. Encouraging children of all ages to be a part of feeding the family teaches them to bring consciousness to cooking and eating. It also opens up a conversation about the *language of food*. Food speaks to us about comfort, desire, decadence, friendship, love, and tradition. Learning your child's food language is important, because it may not be the same as your own.

In my home, we have two vegetarian children and two children who eat meat. They have unfolded these paths on their own, and we help them to honor their own journey with food. Mostly, we want our children to know that food is medicine, providing the life-force that truly nourishes our bodies, minds, and souls.

What messages are you sending to your children about food? Are your children part of understanding the story of food and food traditions in your home? Do you cook together, eat together, and nourish a sacred practice of feeding one another?

REFLECTIONS ⌒

How do you nourish *yourself*? Do you have one standard for yourself and another for your children? Do you eat junk when nobody is around, but insist on healthy eating for your family? What changes do you want to make in the way you nourish your body—the TEMPLE OF YOUR SOUL?

SACRED MOTHERHOOD PRACTICE ⌒

BRING CONSCIOUSNESS AND GRATITUDE TO EVERY MEAL. Before you begin eating and drinking, invite each person to feed another person first, saying, "May you never hunger," and to give them a sip of water, saying, "May you never thirst."

IDEAS ⌒

- "NO FIGHTING IN THE KITCHEN!" We have a rule in our home that nobody can fight in the kitchen. It is considered a sacred space for creating the food we use to nourish each other. Keeping high vibrations in the kitchen infuses the food with positivity and love. While the food itself nourishes the body, the good energy around the food nourishes the soul. Create a "Sacred Space" sign to hang up in your kitchen as a reminder of this intention and practice.

- CREATE A MEALTIME BLESSING. Begin each meal by being thankful for what you have. Use this simple blessing, inspired by a Waldorf kindergarten verse, or create another one that suits your family.

Earth, who gives to us this food,

Sun, who makes it ripe and good,

Dear Earth, Dear Sun,

By you we live.

Our loving thanks to you we give.

Blessings on this meal, and peace on Earth.

PAIRINGS ⌒

- Book: *The Organic Family Cookbook* by Anni Daulter
- Crystal: Clear quartz. When cooking, put a piece of clear quartz

into your pot to raise the pure vibration of the food you are making. Clear quartz is great for increasing purity and seeing clearly. You may consider crystals with other properties if you want to infuse the food you are making with another specific type of healing energy. (Note: Be sure to remove all crystals before serving.)

journal on

Nourish

Reflect here on your relationship
to feeding your family and yourself.
How is food SACRED to you? How
does your family connect around
cooking and eating together? What
food traditions would you like to
nourish in your home?

Sacred Earth

returning to the mother

As the leaves fall and gardens are put to bed, autumn is the season to return to the Earth. It is the time to put down your roots, and remember how to live well in your chosen place. It is the time to celebrate the gifts of the harvest, and offer your thanks. It is the time to feel the ground beneath your feet, and restore your relationship with the sacred Earth Mother.

YOU ᐇ

We are all keenly aware that the Earth is suffering at the hands of the modern human world. Yet it's easy for any mama to get caught up in the daily "to-dos" and lose sight of the disservice she too does to her children—and herself—by falling out of rhythm with the natural world. Our ancient bond to the Earth is our source of sustenance for body and soul.

As you nourish your family with the bounty of the land, it is best to keep your food local and seasonal, and to express your gratitude to Mother Earth with a simple offering or prayer. In this way, you and yours remain embedded in the matrix of life, which in turn enlivens the soul.

Likewise, daily communion with nature attunes the senses and feeds the soul by reawakening *wonder*—the seed of spiritual growth.

YOUR SOUL ᐇ

You are not alone on the sacred path of motherhood. The Earth is your Mother. As you teach your children how to take care of her, remember that she is always there to care for you. Find a special spot in nature that you can visit regularly to cultivate an intimate relationship with the pure nature that is within and around you.

At the beginning of each day, sit on this hallowed ground and tap into the fortifying energy of Earth. When home life turns hectic, take your children to your nature spot to absorb silence and breathe stillness. And when you are in despair, return to Mother Earth and allow her to hold your grief. Lie upon her body and surrender the full weight of your heavy heart. Or dig a hole where you can bury a symbol of your pain, and know that it will be held safely and tenderly.

YOUR CHILD ❧

Nature beckons the soul of every child. It is our birthright to dwell upon this Earth in *right relationship.* Childhood is the time to romp in the woods and discover the delights and mysteries of the natural world. Moreover, there is a growing recognition that nature is essential to the healthy development of mind, body, and spirit. So if your child's hours upon the land are few and far between, make a commitment this week to get your child BACK TO NATURE!

Seasonal nature walks encourage your child's deep-rooted connection to the Earth. Whether you just step outside your back door or make a day trip to some little slice of the wild, spend a few unhurried hours exploring and noticing signs of the season. In fall, observe squirrels stashing food for the winter, or enjoy collecting unusual seedpods. Regularly, and at every time of year, venture out with your child to marvel at the ever-changing face of nature. Your walks will inspire awe and respect for the Earth, and help you to raise a true steward of the land.

REFLECTIONS ❧

Among her countless gifts, the Sacred Earth can serve as a mirror of the cycles in your life, and help you access your inner knowing. The arrangement of this book honors the fact that each time of year reveals different aspects of your being. Likewise, all of the plants, animals, landscapes, and elements reflect various gifts and lessons within you. Greet the Earth Mother, and learn to see yourself in her all manifestations.

SACRED MOTHERHOOD PRACTICE ❧

TAKE A MEDICINE WALK IN NATURE. Draw a line in the dirt, and step across this threshold into a ritual time and space. With heightened awareness and intuition, allow nature to serve as your mirror and teacher. You may wander, sit, pray, dance, throw rocks, or even sleep—everything you do is ceremony, no matter how sacred or profane. Ask a tree for advice, or the wind for a song. Ponder the significance of animal encounters, or bury yourself in the earth. Make your time relevant, mystical, and personal. When you are complete, step back across the threshold, and trust that you received exactly what you needed.

IDEAS

- LEARN THE ART OF COYOTE MENTORING. This educational approach to wilderness awareness uses children's innate enthusiasm for the natural world to develop their capacities for learning, problem-solving, and full expression, and to re-awaken their natural sense of wonder. (See Jon Young's book in "Pairings" below to learn more.)

- CREATE A SEASONAL NATURE TABLE. Designate a special shelf or table for displaying the gifts of the Earth. On a silk or other beautiful cloth, place a few special objects such as wooden figures, beeswax creations, or felted animals, to set a seasonal mood. Invite your children to add their nature finds and handcrafts to celebrate the time of year.

PAIRINGS

- Books: *Last Child in the Woods: Saving Our Children From Nature-Deficit Disorder* by Richard Louv and *Coyote's Guide to Connecting with Nature* by Jon Young, Ellen Haas, and Evan McGown
- Children's book: *52 Nature Activities* by Lynn Gordon
- Music: "Earth's Child" by Mary Isis, and "Earth My Body" by Nicole Sangsuree

Sacred Earth

Write the story of your medicine walk (see "Sacred Motherhood Practice," on page 267), reflecting on the gifts and lessons you received.

Healing

a beautiful journey

Our sorrows and wounds are healed only when we touch them with compassion.
—THE BUDDHA

The beauty of autumn brings with it warmth, love, family, and thoughtful reflection. This comforting sense of safety can also be an invitation to look more closely at your own personal healing path. All of us have wounds that could use some tending. This week we say YES *to loving-up those places that scared us in the past, so that we can befriend them in the present. With deep compassion and courage, we look healing in the eye, and we don't blink.*

YOU

So much of Sacred Motherhood is about looking at the places inside you that are the hardest for you to deal with as a mother. When your children push your buttons, it is worthwhile to dig deep in search of the trigger. Often it is your most tender, unhealed wounds that your children reactivate, causing old defenses and demons to surface in ways that scare everyone, especially you. Motherhood will present opportunity after opportunity to unearth your unconscious wounds, until you finally gather them up and bravely set off down the SACRED PATH OF HEALING.

Becoming a mother can also BE the journey of healing for you. The only true source of healing is LOVE, and while there are many ways to get in touch with love, there is nothing so powerful as the love of a mother for her child. Through your unconditional love and compassion for your little one, you may be able to find healing for yourself—but it is helpful to have a map. Name your wounds, so that you know what you're dealing with. Then draw up a plan for how to manifest healing on a daily basis.

YOUR SOUL

Wounds live deep inside, where it's cozy and warm. They are often hard to uncover, particularly if you are looking to kick them out. If you are harboring any wounds from your own childhood, you'd better believe they will be reopened in moments with your child that recall their pain. This is likely to shake you off of your game, especially if you were not aware that they still hurt.

There may also be lingering physical and/or emotional trauma from the birth of your child, or wounds from your relationship with your mother that get stimulated as you walk your own parenting path. All of these wounds need to be LOVED and HEALED, to unburden your soul of whatever no longer serves you.

Through tears or prayers, ask the universe to help your soul recover from anything and everything that eclipses your own radiance. Visualize healing light shining into any open wound. But remember that it is through your wounds that you may become a healer. It is often your cracks and vulnerabilities that allow DIVINE LOVE to touch your soul. As Rumi reminds us, "The wound is the place where Light enters you."

YOUR CHILD ❧

Your child may have entered the world with ancestral or karmic wounds; she may have experienced trauma at birth, or she may be hurting from childhood experiences beyond your control. You are there to tend her wounds with care, to hold sacred space for her self-healing, to guide her, and to help her find meaning on any healing path she may walk.

Does your child cry or get angry a lot? Rather than reacting negatively, ask the universe to help you see what kind of healing she needs. Work with her in a tender way as she experiences the pain of internal or external hurts. Wrap your arms around her, show her LOVE, tell her she is LOVED and that she is a reflection of PURE LOVE, and remind her that the places where her heart hurts can be healed with LOVE.

REFLECTIONS ❧

Do you know and understand the places within you that need to be healed? Take time to really sit with what needs to be healed within you, so that you do not unconsciously pass your wounds on to your child. Some of your wounds may have come down through your family, generation after generation. You have the power to heal the wounds within you, so that your own child may not have to carry such a heavy load.

SACRED MOTHERHOOD PRACTICE ⚮

CREATE A HEALING MANTRA. Try repeating, "I heal all my inner wounds with love," or make up one that speaks directly to your situation. Then take just a few minutes before you get out of bed every morning to say your healing mantra to yourself, at least five times, with mindful breaths between repetitions.

IDEAS ⚮

· DIVINE YOUR HEALING PATH. Grab a divination deck or pack of inspirational cards. *The Mother's Wisdom Deck* is perfect for this, as it speaks directly to the experience of motherhood. Light a small candle, ask for help in healing any lingering past wounds, and pull a card. Then turn to the guidebook for more insight into the meaning of the card you drew as it relates to your own healing journey.

· MAKE A CHILD'S HEALING BASKET. As the go-to place for everyday healing, fill a special basket with Rescue Remedy, first-aid cream, bandages, tweezers, and a selection of healing salves, tinctures, and remedies, which you can either make or buy at a natural-foods store. Add some special hand cream or lip balm that your child loves, to help engage them in their own self-healing as you tend to the bumps and scrapes.

PAIRINGS ⚮

· Children's song: "Long Time Sun" by Snatam Kaur
· Crystal: Chrysoprase is a heart-centric stone that encourages deep healing. It can be used alone or together with other crystals to help heal more effectively.

- Herbal Ally: Make Healing Heart Tea to enjoy during your inspirational card reading.

HEALING HEART TEA

2 parts rose petals

1 part dried skullcap flowers

1 part hawthorn berries

1 part oat straw

Combine herbs and steep in freshly boiled water in a muslin bag or tea ball/infuser.

- Sacred Living Movement Retreat: Mama's Sacred Medicine Cupboard (online)

journal on

Healing

Take a deep look at the wounds you carry. Where did they come from? When and how do they resurface? And what can you do to begin healing them?

_____

_____

_____

_____

_____

_____

_____

_____

_____

_____

_____

_____

_____

_____

_____

forgiveness

rip + release

Beauty looks like encouragement, patience, acceptance, forgiveness, carefulness, and compassion.
—ERYKAH BADU

Forgiveness comes to light in the golden glow of autumn, beckoning us to raise our hearts and lighten our loads. As much as it encourages us to move toward the light, it also challenges us to dive deep into the darker places within. This week, entertain both possibilities, granting yourself sacred space for opening up and letting go of past pains. We all hold onto things that have deeply wounded us, but if we can liberate this pain from the past, we are free to live in peace.

YOU ॐ

The weak can never forgive. Forgiveness is the attribute of the strong.
—GANDHI

We all have been wronged. On the "crappy things that happen to us" scale, however, some things are far weightier than others. The problem with the heavier, more burdensome transgressions is that they can turn into balls of anger and resentment that lodge inside your body and suffocate your soul. In fact, they can become so big and oppressive that they can move you off of your destined path and start to consume you, especially when they are really big monsters of hurt.

I know that forgiving someone who has deeply hurt you is easier said than done, but I will ask you to do it anyway. Here's why: Holding onto anger and pain from the past keeps you chained to the past, and energetically tied to the person who wronged you. This does not serve you! Forgiving someone for hurting you is not the same as saying that what happened is okay—it just releases you from having to bear the suffering any longer. When you choose not to forgive the person who hurt you, you continue to hurt yourself every day by rehashing and perpetuating the energy of the transgression.

Now that you are a mother, your time and energy is more precious than ever. Don't waste it on reliving past wounds! Live in the present with *love, trust, and possibility* in your heart.

YOUR SOUL ❧

Pains that live in your soul hurt your auric body. This means that they attack the life-force that cycles through you, and can end up causing physical manifestations of your emotional and spiritual wounding. That means you could get sick if you don't LET GO of all that crappy stuff. If you feel physically weak, out of balance, and depleted, consider looking to your emotional and spiritual bodies for some answers. You will want to also maintain physical practices that keep your body healthy—but remember that you are a holistic woman in which mind, body, and spirit coexist and interrelate. Practicing forgiveness unencumbers your soul, making way for serenity, love, and life-force to move in and around you, delivering *happiness and health.*

YOUR CHILD ❧

Your children look to you for how to be in the world. What a massive responsibility! You have to have queen-like behavior in order to show your little ones how to be NOBLE. If you forgive them their trespasses, then they will learn to forgive others. If you are gentle with yourself when you make mistakes, they will be gentle with themselves. And if your children witness an argument between you and your partner, be sure they also witness your sincere apologies and loving reconciliation. This will offer guideposts by which they can navigate disagreements in their own relationships.

Last but not least—even though these bighearted little beings naturally forgive their mamas' missteps and oversights—when you make a mistake at your child's expense be sure to say you are sorry. It is okay for your children to see you as human; just take responsibility for yourself so they can *trust* you and also learn that they deserve to be treated with *respect and kindness.*

REFLECTIONS ❧

The flip side to forgiving others is to forgive yourself for wronging another, or for simply not being perfect. Often this is the hardest thing of all. Take some time to look at your list of wrongs, and see how you can offer up a healthy dose of compassion to yourself. Are you able to forgive yourself? You are human, after all, and will make many mistakes in life. You must have compassion for yourself in order to extend it to others. And you must forgive yourself in order to offer forgiveness to others.

SACRED MOTHERHOOD PRACTICES ⊙⌒

VISUALIZE FORGIVENESS. Take some time to reflect on what you need to forgive and heal within yourself. Then write these things down. When you're ready, sit in a quiet space and give yourself some time for this guided visualization (compliments of Sue Crowder from the Sacred Self-Love program):

> *Picture yourself walking across a beautiful field of wildflowers carrying these heavy things with you—perhaps dragging them behind you because they are so hard to hold. When you cross the field, you come to a ledge overlooking a swiftly flowing river. Pick up your heavy burdens and, one by one, throw them into the river. Imagine that you watch them flow down the river, until the current swallows them.*
>
> *These things are no longer yours to carry. You've let them go, and now you will be able to heal a piece of yourself. As you walk back across the field of wildflowers, pick a few to carry home with you. Enjoy the natural beauty of the world. Notice how much lighter you feel without carrying the burden of a heavy heart. Allow yourself to feel the joy of a heart on the mend.*

IDEAS ⊙⌒

- CREATE A FALL FORGIVENESS TREE. Draw the outline of a tree, and upon each leaf write the name of someone you need to forgive. One by one, work with each leaf: Perhaps write a note of forgiveness, or simply write, "I forgive you" on a piece of paper and burn it. If you feel the need, and if it would be a kindness to the other person, you can reach out to the person who hurt you and release negative feelings that way. As you complete the forgiveness process represented by each leaf, decorate it until you have a tree—and a heart!—full of light and color. Don't worry if it takes you a long time to finish; forgiveness doesn't happen overnight.

- RIP + RELEASE. Take a few colorful squares of raw silk that you can rip into strips. Begin each strip by nicking the cloth with scissors, but then LET 'ER RIP, and as you do so, release one past hurt that you have been carrying around. Then tie one end of each strip onto a string to make a banner of forgiveness that you can hang outside, fluttering freely in the wind and letting it carry the old hurts far away.

pairings ☙

- Children's song: "The Sun Shines on Everyone" by Snatam Kaur
- Crystal: Rhodochrosite boosts self-love and compassion, and supports healing of past wounds. Use this stone when working with forgiveness, by holding it in your palm as you do the release work described in this section.
- Music: "Hallelujah" by MaMuse

journal on

*f*orgiveness

Make some notes here about forgiveness: Who is on your "need to
forgive" list? What past wounds are
you ready to surrender? On a separate piece of paper, write a letter to someone you need to forgive.
Describe all the ways they have hurt you. Get it all out, once and for
all. And then forgive them, burn your letter—and let it all go!

_____
_____
_____
_____
_____
_____
_____
_____
_____
_____
_____
_____
_____

Storytelling

*weaving a web
for the soul*

Around the time of Halloween and the Celtic observance of Samhain, when the veils between the worlds are said to be their thinnest and magic is afoot, stories come alive! *We hunker down by the fire, whispering tales of old and spinning yarns about our younger days. Like a web, these stories catch up our little ones, holding them close and speaking the language of the soul. This week, as the darkest time of the year begins, we summon stories to enchant our homes and live in our bones.*

YOU ☙

We all have a story to tell. Some folks are natural storytellers; they can turn a trip to the dentist into an epic adventure. Others need to have their stories drawn out of them with the help of a good prompt or a patient friend. Whatever your storytelling bent, *your stories need to be told.* Only when they leave your safekeeping can they be tied together with lines from other lives, mooring your voice and experience to the shared story of humanity, and assuring us all that we are not alone in this vast ocean of existence.

What is your story? Do your childhood tales speak of happiness or woe? When did you first fall in love? How might you describe your feats of daring and strength? Though your story can be hard to put into words, it will take on a life of its own as soon as you muster the courage to open your mouth or start moving your pen. There is beauty in stark honesty, and a freedom that comes from baring all. As your story begins to unfurl, the effort to hold it in begins to relax, making space for you to step back and gain perspective before writing your chapter on motherhood.

YOUR SOUL ☙

We are constantly rewriting our stories—editing details, introducing characters, and redirecting the plot. But sometimes we get stuck. Have you ever become overly attached to your story? Not the deep, mythic, soul-feeding kind of story, but the automatic, superficial account of what's right and wrong in your life? Did you share it with everyone who would listen, until you eventually grew tired of hearing your own tired tale? If so, listen up.

The stories you tell shape the life you live. In the mothering years, it is easy to fall into a rut of focusing on hardship and toil. "How was your day, dear?" begets "You wouldn't believe the shit I went through!" But is this the storyline you truly want to follow? See it for what it is—a string of beliefs, perceptions, and explanations you have been clinging to, in an attempt to make sense of your frustrations and your yearnings. While a litany of complaints may feel like a truthful account of some days, it is not your deepest *truth*.

When this gloomy tale puts you in a box, it's time to bust out and pick up the thread of a deeper story—one that *mirrors your soul*. How? Pick up a journal, and scribble out all your grumbles and grievances. Write without stopping, until you start to hear a different voice telling of the beauty found in ordinary things, and resurrecting the original mythos of your spiritual quest.

YOUR CHILD ⌒

There is nothing like candlelight and a wide-eyed child to deliver you into the land of stories. As you begin to remember the eternal nature of your story, you may be drawn to the fathomless well of age-old myths, fables, and fairytales. These stories not only mirror your archetypal journey, they also speak directly to your child's soul, invoking a full range of imaginal experiences and rooting them in the common ground we all walk as humans.

Some stories invite you and your child to fully appreciate the magic of the everyday world. Others reflect the experience of a young child leaving the nest for the first time to encounter the world and then return to the safety of home. Still others meet growing children as they pick up the keys to their own kingdoms, test boundaries like a classic trickster, or slay dragons to recover a treasure that is in fact their own *pure heart*.

REFLECTIONS ᐒ

There are countless ways to tap this wellspring of universal wisdom with your family. You may be called to let stories live through you as a storyteller. You may wish to write healing tales to help ease your child's proverbial growing pains. You may be inspired to make costumes and step into a particularly powerful story through a live performance. And Halloween, of course, is the perfect time for everyone to embody a favorite alter ego.

SACRED MOTHERHOOD PRACTICE ᐒ

REWRITE YOUR STORY. This week, bring your awareness to how you narrate the movements of your day. Are you empowered by the story you tell? If not, how can you edit a sentence or two to weave in more *beauty* and *soul food?*

IDEAS ᐒ

- BECOME A STORYTELLER. Children love any story you tell them, especially if it has anything to do with supernatural beings, secret worlds, or your childhood pets. Try putting them to bed with a serial story about boys and girls *just like themselves,* who have all kinds of wild adventures and special powers, to seed their dreams with possibility.

- WRITE WITH WISE WOMEN. Start a writing group to gather the stories of your tribe. Research some provocative prompts to help the writing get started, or choose a line from a favorite poem. Write for a predetermined amount of time, without pausing to censor or edit. Then share your stories aloud, and serve as sacred witness to the beauty and power coming through one another's stories.

PAIRINGS ᐒ

- Books: *Start Where You Are: A Journal for Self-Exploration* by Meera Lee Patel and *Healing Stories for Challenging Behavior* by Susan Perrow
- Children's book: *Tell Me a Story: Mystery in the Forest* (and other creative story-card sets) by eeBoo

Pick a chapter in your life, and begin writing the *epic* of your becoming.

_____

_____

_____

_____

_____

_____

_____

_____

_____

_____

_____

_____

_____

_____

_____

_____

_____

Dreamtime

resting in the void

Following active summer days, fall offers a welcome respite. Cooler days invite you to turn inward and sit in reverie. Longer nights leave more time for wandering in the dreamtime. Take time in this season to slow down and REST IN THE VOID.

YOU ⌒

What is your relationship to the dreamtime? Most importantly, are you getting enough sleep? All of us mamas could do with a few more winks, but sleep deprivation should not be a badge of motherhood. Without enough rest to restore yourself during the night, you cannot be fully present, let alone joyful, during the day. If the dark circles under your eyes are becoming a permanent fixture, it is high time to reset your sleep cycles.

Be committed and creative. Try a new family sleeping arrangement based on what works best for you, rather than on a book or a friend's advice. Ask your partner to help with the night shift, if needed. And nap whenever you can, even if laundry is piling up. Sleep is not a luxury; it is a necessity!

YOUR SOUL ⌒

If you are getting adequate sleep, you should spend about a third of your life in the dreamtime. Not only do we sleep to replenish our bodies, we sleep in order to *dream*. Whether you are a prolific dreamer or rarely recall your nighttime visions, you do in fact dream each night. In the dream-state, your soul is free to wander in mysterious realms and return with wisdom for your waking life.

Remembering your dreams offer access to this reservoir of insight. To develop dream recall, keep a dream journal by your bed and record your dreams—even those informative little dream fragments—as soon as you awake. When you open your eyes, do not move or let thoughts of the day ahead nudge the dream out of your awareness. Replay the dream in your mind, and then write it down in detail. Finally, trust your intuition to interpret the messages that your dreams deliver from this rich *inner* and *other* world.

YOUR CHILD ❧

Your children live closer to the dreamtime than you do; most children spend about half their lives asleep. Whether your child fights the transition from waking to sleeping or effortlessly drifts off, nighttime rituals can help open the gateway to a magical dream realm. Have fun creating a bedtime ritual that is special and relaxing for all. Perhaps begin with a soothing lavender-oil bath, or a calming cup of chamomile tea. Then snuggle into bed for a quiet bedtime story—just one is most conducive to sleep—and a lullaby by candlelight. Close the day and open the night by blowing out the candle with a mother's blessing of love and *sweet dreams*.

When your little ones awake from their slumber, you can encourage dream awareness by sharing your dreams, and listening attentively for what theirs may reveal. Children's dreams tend to be prolific, and can bring to light whatever is scary, worrying, or intriguing to them. Inviting your child to make a dream pillow or dream catcher with you is another wonderful way to honor and activate dream life.

REFLECTIONS ❧

Dreaming unfolds in the daytime as well as at night. Some of us are more prone to staring out the window, and seldom is this tendency applauded. This week, celebrate the DAYDREAMER in you! Consider playing hooky from school or work, with the intention of simply sleeping in and zoning out. When we take a break, our unconscious mind can get to work. Deep knowing can bubble up from the void, taking us even further along our path than when we are busy exerting ourselves.

SACRED MOTHERHOOD PRACTICE ❧

PRACTICE THE SACRED ART OF DREAM INCUBATION. Before you go to sleep, set an intention to have meaningful dreams, and to remember them. Solicit your inner dreamer to bring you a powerful, clear, and visionary dream. You might even pose a specific question, or ask for healing from the dream world. As you close your eyes, hold gratitude for the dreamer in you.

IDEAS ⌒⌒

- MAKE DREAM PILLOWS WITH YOUR CHILD. Take two 8 x 8-inch squares of soft natural fabric, place them face-to-face, and sew them together along three sides. Create a custom blend of your favorite dream-inducing, dried herbs using catnip for deep sleep, chamomile to ward off bad dreams, lavender for relaxation, mugwort to enhance dreaming, and rosemary for dream recall. Turn your pillow rightside-out, and loosely fill with your about a cupful of your fragrant botanical mixture. Sew up the opening, and bring your pillow to bed.

- CREATE DREAM CATCHERS TO SUSPEND ABOVE YOUR BEDS. Dream catchers originated among the Ojibwe people, whose magical woven-string webs catch bad dreams and allow only good dreams to pass through a hole in the center. To make your own dream catcher, find a flexible willow branch and fashion it into a circle. Then follow an online resource for directions to weave the web. As you weave, you can add beads and other decorative or symbolic items. Finish it off by hanging a feather from the bottom of the hoop, to guide the good dreams down to the dreamer below. Hang it above where you sleep.

PAIRINGS ⌒⌒

- Book: *Buddha at Bedtime: Tales of Love and Wisdom for You to Read with Your Child to Enchant, Enlighten, and Inspire* by Dharmachari Nagaraja
- Children's music: "Lullaby," by Jewel, and "Meditation for Kids" by Sada
- Crystal: Azurite resonates with the third-eye chakra, helping you open up to guidance from the dreamtime and the otherworld. Tuck a piece under your pillow to enhance your dreams and support dream interpretation.

journal on

Dreamtime

This week, use this space to record your dreams. Keep this book by your bed to catch any dream snippets just as you awake.

Shadow + Light

may the two meet
in prayer

Where there is darkness, there is also light. It's the yin and yang of life. To walk the mindful path of mothering, you must be willing to honor both, because mother-hood cracks you open to both deep discomfort and supreme joy—sometimes in the same moment. It is this complex dance of shadow and light that reflects who you are; neither alone can tell the complete story. This week, as if in prayer, we bring the two halves together to sing praises for your WHOLENESS.

YOU ℮⌣

If you are going to be cracked open to the full experience of mother-hood, you have to believe that you are *strong* enough and *sacred* enough to hold it all—the light, the dark, and every nuanced shade of gray. Above all, you must face and embrace the blackest fear that something may happen to your child. This is a special brand of fear that only a mother can fully grasp, and it can be paralyzing at times.

On the other end of the spectrum, you are blessed to live with these mini-reflections of yourself. As your greatest teachers, your children know how to bring you to your knees, while simultaneously shining as the brightest star you've ever seen.

When you step onto the path of motherhood, you dive deeper into yourself than ever before, uncovering shadowy places you never even knew existed. Do not be afraid of your darker side! Pushing it away will only make it more fearful and powerful. Instead, welcome your shadow self as an old friend, and learn what she has to teach you about being human. Her wisdom will help you show up as a more compassionate, authentic, and *whole* mother.

YOUR SOUL ℮⌣

Stuff happens in life—great stuff, and crappy stuff. *All* of it informs and shapes the many facets of your being. At times, some past experience may take on a life of its own and overwhelm your conscious mind. Based on your past, you may live from a reactive place, with-out being fully aware of what's going on deep inside you. When you have children, this can get compounded further by a tiny human often wanting things from you that you may not be able to give.

The trick to healing these shadow aspects is not to mask, hide, repress, or deny them. Instead, you must shine light on whatever is lurking in the corners of your psyche, so that you can truly understand and *integrate* all aspects of who you are. This shifts the pattern of unconscious, reactive living to informed, mindful living, which supports healing and the possibility of transformation. Shadow and light exist as one; they cannot be separated. Like lovers bound by passion, they must know each other intimately to exist at all. Embrace *both!*

YOUR CHILD ༄

When your children are babies, they are so innocent and pure that it is hard to imagine them ever doing anything "bad." Then they grow, and while they gather giggles and love to store in their hearts, they also gather hurts and upsets that take up residence inside them as well. Children cannot fully process everything that happens to them, nor do they have as many ways to filter their behaviors. Therefore they may react or discharge their feelings in ways that challenge adult sensibilities—but are in fact very healthy. They may also speak blunt truths about their wounds and shadow selves.

Honor these places within them, and nurture the tender moments when these hard truths meet the light of day. While you may want to protect your children from ever feeling pain and discomfort, remember that their dharmic paths are dappled with both light and shadow. They must find a way through it all, to fulfill their destinies.

REFLECTIONS ༄

How do you find yourself? You *look,* seeking both the shadow and the light that together make up your wholeness. Shadow and light allow you to be who you truly are, in every moment. Can you greet your shadow side right now, with love?

SACRED MOTHERHOOD PRACTICES ❧

LOVE *ALL* OF WHO YOU ARE. For one week, refrain from making negative comments about yourself to anyone. Mark it on your calendar, and everyday when you wake up, set an intention to only uplift yourself and those around you. Deepen the practice by withholding judgment of others, transforming these thoughts into compassion and acceptance.

IDEAS ❧

- RELEASE IT! Go to an open body of water. Sit and stare at the expansiveness, and then find two rocks. On one rock, write what you want to release from yourself, yell it to the universe, and throw it into the water. On the other rock, write what you want to empower in yourself, and take that rock home with you. Every morning and evening, hold the rock and speak your empowerment *out loud*.

- PRAY FOR INTEGRATION. The Anjali Mudra brings spirit and matter together as you bring your open, flat hands together, pointing upward, into the classic prayer pose in front of your heart. As your palms come together, they symbolize the self meeting the greater Self. Practice this mudra and honor your wholeness through prayer.

PAIRINGS ❧

- Crystal: Aventurine is an all-purpose healer and balancer. When you feel your shadow is out of balance, this stone can help you find equilibrium. Consider wearing aventurine as jewelry, or carrying it with you at all times, particularly when you feel stressed.

- Music: "Witches" by Cowboy Junkies, and "Hold It All" by Red Molly

Shadow + Light

Explore the light and dark within you. Start by listing three shadow aspects of yourself, and three light aspects. How does each of these serve you, or sabotage you? How do they each contribute to your growth and deep soul-work? What work do you need to do to integrate them all into WHOLENESS?

_____

_____

_____

_____

_____

_____

_____

_____

_____

_____

_____

_____

_____

_____

_____

Passages

honoring change

Leaves are turning, and a new school year has begun, making fall an obvious harbinger of CHANGE. *But this time of year also beckons you to look deeper, with an eye to the inner transformations that are afoot.*

YOU ☙

In the sea of change that is motherhood, it can be hard to keep your head above water. Daily changes are detectable in your small, chrysalis-like beings as they bravely evolve into butterflies. Changes like potty training are welcome, while others—such as talking back to mom as an expression of newfound independence—not so much. And you? You have to hold your heart-center while shape-shifting to greet every age and stage.

At each new turn, a practice of letting go and mourning may allow you to fully embrace the evolutionary reality of your children's lives. Every year on my children's birthdays, I feel overwhelmed by nostalgia for the baby or toddler or child to whom I am bidding farewell. I shed a few tears, and only then am I ready to celebrate the radiant child who stands before me now.

How do you roll with changes? Did weaning break your heart? What about the first day of kindergarten, or college? Or are you enlivened by the fact that the only constant is change?

YOUR SOUL ☙

Aside from the everyday flow of changes that comes with motherhood, major passages in life including birth, menarche, marriage, motherhood, menopause, and death are accompanied by a life-changing metamorphosis. As you navigate these permanent transformations in your children and yourself, RITES OF PASSAGE offer solace and sustenance at the level of the soul. Whether traditional or contemporary, these rituals provide a container for the chaos and celebration of change by helping us first SEPARATE from an old way of being, then move through a betwixt-and-between state of TRANSITION, and finally to CLAIM a new position in the grand scheme of things.

Rites of passage take many forms. Open to the limitless possibilities by looking to your cultural roots as well as new expressions of age-old rites. Have fun exploring Blessing Ways, Baby Blessings, Bar/Bat Mitzvahs, and more. What feels authentic to you? Can you tap into rites of passage that are already alive and well in your community? Or are you called to create new rituals to usher yourself, your family, or your tribe through pivotal moments in the cycle of life?

YOUR CHILD ᶜ⌒ͻ

Milestones in every child's life are worthy of celebration. They call attention to the growth and vitality of our children, and give us pause to count our blessings. Some, like the arrival or loss of a first tooth, can be marked with sweet and simple celebrations. Coming-of-age, on the other hand, calls for a momentous honoring event, as your spirited adolescent leaves childhood and stands precariously on the threshold of adulthood. It is never too early to beginning planting the seeds of intention for these poignant moments. You will likely be surprised how quickly they arrive.

Awareness of your children's soul development can deliver strength and grace, should you encounter an uncomfortable growing edge. In a changing six-year-old, for example, you can anticipate alternating bouts of clinginess and autonomy, while the nine-year-old asks for you to hold strong, loving boundaries as your child seeks more self-determination. If you find yourself in unfamiliar territory, dig around to glean wisdom from those who have come before you. But—most importantly—trust that you will know when to hold your children teetering on the verge of a leap of faith, and when to gently push them to spread their wings and *fly*.

REFLECTIONS ᶜ⌒ͻ

Review the major turning points in your life. Were they honored and celebrated, or not? What highlights would you like to recreate with your family? What major life moments would you like to honor in a different, more sacred manner?

SACRED MOTHERHOOD PRACTICE ❧

CREATE A RITE OF PASSAGE. Identify one major passage that is on the horizon for you or someone you love. Create a beautiful ritual of saying goodbye to the old, transitioning through the unknown, and claiming the new. There are many beautiful, powerful, and symbolic choices to incorporate in your ritual. You can bless and burn, pray and praise, dance and drum.

IDEAS ❧

- SAY GOODBYE IN A SACRED MANNER. When a pet dies, support your child in celebrating and grieving. Make a list of everything they have enjoyed and will miss about this special friend. Read it aloud, and let the tears flow. Then release the beloved by burying the list, along with a special token of your love. Be sure to sing, light candles, and *make it sacred.*

- TURN TO THE MOON. Using the "Grandmother Moon Spread" in *The Mother's Wisdom Deck,* pull four cards to illuminate tides of change: one represents waning energy; one reflects the Mystery; one mirrors the awakening self; and one represents the full light of this new becoming.

PAIRINGS ❧

- Books: *How to Bury a Goldfish: And Other Ceremonies & Celebrations for Everyday Life* by Virginia Lang and Louise Nayer and *Living Passages for the Whole Family: Celebrating Rites of Passage from Birth to Adulthood* by Shea Darian

journal on

Passages

What changes are stirring in your life right now? What are you ready to let go of, in order to claim a new you? What kind of ritual might support this sacred metamorphosis?

Gratitude + Abundance

celebrating your bounty

This season, make time to honor your personal harvest. Take a long, grateful look at the big picture of what you have manifested throughout the year—but also find ways to celebrate the smaller blessings, so that you don't miss the nuances of abundance that help you thrive everyday.

Happiness and abundance arise from the gratitude that lives in your heart. If you are not appreciating your current bounty—which includes all you have, and all you have become—then your heart knows little joy, because you live in a state of perpetual wanting. Ultimately, this wanting leads to suffering and attachment, and inhibits the flow of energy and opportunity into your life. This week, we will look at how gratitude is the path of ABUNDANCE.

YOU ⟳

The first step toward living in abundance is BELIEVING that you are always, and in all ways, provided for! This allows you to live in gratitude for all that you have, and to GIVE, even when you think you can't. With an abundance mindset, you understand that there really is enough to go around, and can see yourself and your life as a natural part of this circle of plenty.

As a mother, it's especially important to understand the energetics of gratitude and abundance, so that you can consciously pass this wisdom on to your little ones. If you live in a sense of lack and fear that the well will run dry, you will mother from a place that is tight instead of relaxed, stressed instead of free, closed to opportunities instead of open to them. And your oh-so-perceptive children will sense your contraction, especially when you are worried about the flow of resources (e.g., money).

Why not try giving and receiving from a place of abundance and gratitude instead? This will shift your relationship to prosperity, and create an energy wherein all things are possible for you and your family. You have the power to foster a healthy relationship with money, so that your children can learn about staying in a state of positive, abundant flow throughout their lives.

YOUR SOUL ❧

Another step on the path of BOUNTY is to truly believe that you are WORTHY of living an abundant life. Vibrant abundance is the nature of things. Look to the rich manifestation of Mother Earth as she gives freely to all the beings that walk upon her soils and fly in her skies.

You too are *enough!* If you cannot truly take this to heart, take care to nurture and heal any parts within you that may not feel worthy. Proclaiming your intrinsic worth is an essential part of living in wholehearted gratitude and attracting everything you need. It allows you to fully embrace your YES and say that you are ready for abundance and prosperity.

Now bring in the bounty, sweetheart! Begin each morning by creating a space where gratitude fills your heart. Feel thankfulness pulsating within you as you look at your children and know that you are rich in love and faith. With this as the truest reflection of your soul, you are capable of having the abundance you desire. The possibilities are infinite!

YOUR CHILD ❧

Fortunately, children are naturally tuned to trust the flow of abundance—they have no choice in the matter. A baby does not choose to trust that his mother will feed and hug him; he can only trust that she will. When all goes well, and this trust builds up over time, the child's openness to the flow of abundance expands. He expects things to appear whenever he needs them, even while beginning to explore a wider world. This innocent state of receptivity is the very space in which manifestation can happen.

So look to your children, if you want to learn how to live in natural abundance. Opening to magic and possibility like a child does will allow you to understand the very "how" and "why" of energy flow. Children get it, without even trying! Nurture this deep wisdom in your children, and pray they don't lose it. It serves as a beacon, lighting up the roads of abundance that grownups get lost trying to find, time and time again. A child's trusting map is all you need to understand the simple laws of abundance.

REFLECTIONS ❧

While it's important to rally appreciation for others, it's equally important to do the same for yourself! There is only one you, and you are creating your *legacy* right here and now. What will it be? Cultivating a life of gratitude is a *huge* gift you can leave to your children and the world. But it all begins with you—self-love is the key to spiritual, emotional, and physical gold.

You have the ability to live in abundance, but you must understand first how it works, and second how to apply it to your life. Do you withhold abundance from yourself? Do you say NO to yourself more than you say YES? This is valuable information, and once you know something you can't un-know it. Allow honesty to be a big part of this conversation with yourself: How truly grateful are you for *you*?

SACRED MOTHERHOOD PRACTICES ❧

EXPAND YOUR GRATITUDE. Up the ante on the gratitude practice described in Week 3. Every morning, instead of naming three things for which you are grateful, choose just one—but make it something *new* each day. See how many days you can go before you exhaust your gratitude, holding open the possibility that your gratitude may expand *infinitely*.

IDEAS

- RELEASE LACK. Take a bay leaf, and write the word "lack" on it. When you feel totally ready to release your attachment to lack, *burn it!* If the leaf crackles and burns brightly, then the outcome is positive, and you really were ready to release your attachment to a state of lack. If it smolders, then the outcome is negative, and lack continues to live somewhere within you. If this is the case, work on freeing this energy by withholding less, and saying YES more often. Eventually, try burning another leaf and see what happens.

- ANOINT YOURSELF WITH ABUNDANCE. Create some Abundance Oil, and apply a drop or two to your forehead every day as you work with gratitude and manifestation.

ABUNDANCE OIL

3 oz. apricot oil

3 drops ginger root essential oil

2 drops orange essential oil

Shaving of orange peel

4 drops pine essential oil

2 drops cinnamon essential oil

A few small pieces of cinnamon

2 drops rose essential oil

A few rose petals

2 drops chamomile essential oil

A few whole chamomile flowers

2 drops cedarwood essential oil

5 drops jasmine or lotus essential oil

1 small piece of citrine (a yellow quartz)

1 pinch gold flakes

Fill a four-ounce glass bottle ¾ full of apricot oil and then add the other ingredients to make this potent potion.

---

pairings

- Children's book: *The Table Where Rich People Sit* by Byrd Baylor, illustrated by Peter Parnall
- Music: "Kinder" by Copper Wimmin

journal on

Gratitude + Abundance

Reflect on your relationship to abundance and gratitude. Do you live in fear and a sense of lack, or do you thrive in openness and abundance?
What steps can you take to welcome more *bounty* into your life?

_____

_____

_____

_____

_____

_____

_____

_____

_____

_____

_____

_____

_____

_____

Winter

Mind

Compassion

Tribe

Presence

Tradition

Reflection

Structure

Pine

Respect

Cozy Sweaters

Giving

Commitment

Twinkle Lights

Sovereignty

Snow Flakes

Connection

Right Speech

Right Action

Empowerment

Celebration

creating epic moments

Until further notice, celebrate everything!
—UNKNOWN

In winter, when there is more darkness than light, our impulse is to gather togeth-er. It's as if we come together because we want to light up the world with candles, baking, singing, and praying. As our actions wrap beauty and warmth around everything and everyone, the everyday is made sacred. This week, in the wintertime spirit of celebration, we look at how we can bring family and friends together with intention, to create EPIC MOMENTS *in a Beauty Way.*

YOU ⌒

What were family celebrations like in your home when you were grow-ing up? Did you enjoy them? Were they filled with laughter and love—or were they a sure place for family feuds to rear their ugly heads?

Depending on whether or not these were feel-good times, you may have traditions that you are joyfully carrying down through the generations, or you may be creating new celebrations to reflect your family and your beliefs, now that you are the mama-master of cer-emonies. When it comes to celebration, there are only a few rules: It should feel magical; it should feel meaningful; and it should feel sacred to *you*.

As you follow these guidelines, your family celebrations will come to reflect your beliefs, and transform your everyday world into a sacred playground. Dress up, decorate, light candles, make special foods, play music, and step into ceremony. No matter how you mark special times of year and life, one thing is for certain—each time you invite your family into celebration and ceremony, you create magical moments that your children will hold like treasures for the rest of their days.

When I started my own family, I decided that some of the tradi-tional celebrations did not suit me anymore. We have started our own unique traditions around the solstices and equinoxes, and also introduced special mini-holidays including half-birthdays and full moons that we celebrate throughout the year, helping us remember that life is *always* sacred.

YOUR SOUL ℰ⌢

Why wait to celebrate the blessings of this sacred life? Why not make it a daily practice? A celebration meets the soul in joyous ways, and sinks in as a lasting memory that ignites your pleasure centers. You can elevate the everyday in small ways, so that you live in your Ceremonial Mind more often than anywhere else. This is the mind of *intention, gratitude, and possibility.*

Ceremonial Mind says that every moment is sacred. It transforms mundane tasks into intentional living. We enter Ceremonial Mind when we create a space with care and thoughtful intention, and when we choose to be alive and absorbed in the moment. This commitment to the present makes time *timeless,* and everything becomes a celebration! This is the magic of the in-between moments—the ones that we think don't count, but that actually add up to living a sacred, ceremonial, Beauty-Way, EPIC life.

YOUR CHILD ℰ⌢

There is nothing children like better than a good party! The excitement of the buildup, planning, and preparation brings a thrill to a child's small world. Joyful anticipation resounds throughout the home until the doorbell rings with the first guest's arrival. Celebrating with children reminds us to *have fun,* delight in simple pleasures, and share the blessings of life with others. Children love to be a part of making others feel good and chime with laughter on special days.

Help your children to also bring beauty and enjoyment to everyday sacred living. At mealtime, you can invite them to set the table in a Beauty Way, using cloth napkins, silverware, a flower arrangement, and a candle. Or create a Sacred Space together in your home for reflection and meditation: Set up a simple altar with a candle, crystals, inspirational cards, and perhaps a singing bowl.

When you pass down these simple traditions to your children, they will integrate them as a part of the fabric of who they are. Small but EPIC moments will shape them into the adults you hope they will become.

REFLECTIONS ℮ↄ

Open yourself up to reflect on what celebration means to you. Take a look back at the celebrations you have participated in throughout your life: What meaning do they hold for you? Were they all you had hoped they would be? How might you choose to do things a little differently with your own family? This is a time and a place for you to uncover your thoughts about celebration, and unwrap the gifts that live within yourself to mark the transitions in your home in your own chosen ways.

SACRED MOTHERHOOD PRACTICE ℮ↄ

TAKE ON A SACRED MISSION. Take on one thing that you can easily do each day to bring intention, ceremony, and celebration to an everyday moment. You could light a candle at every meal, day and night. Or, you could wake up early each morning to sing the sun into the sky. Whatever you choose to do, make *sacred* your mission in life.

IDEAS ℮ↄ

· MAKE UP YOUR OWN FAMILY CELEBRATIONS. Create a few new traditions or mini-holidays that you can sprinkle throughout the year to make your family life more sacred and special. Here are a couple of ideas—make up some of your own too!

· FULL MOON COOKIES—On the full moon, bake cookies (moon shapes are great!) and place one outside in the moonlight for the full-moon fairies to take home. In return, they will leave a special little note and/or maybe a little crystal, or a small, round, white stone, or some other moon-themed nature gift for all the children in the home.

- YULE LOG—Get a log of any size, and decorate it with holly, cinnamon sticks, elderberries, pine, cedar, and whatever other combustible items call to you. Write up a family intention that expresses your collective aspirations for the coming year; tuck that into the log too. On Winter Solstice, burn the log, as a way of celebrating the return of the light and firing up family's vision for a bright future.

pairings ⌒

- Books: *Circle Round* by Starhawk, *Festivals, Family, and Food* by Diana Carry and Julie Large and *Naturally Fun Parties For Kids* by Anni Daulter, with Heather Fontenot
- Music: "Beautiful Life" by Nick Fradiani

journal on
Celebration

Use this space to plan a CELEBRA-
TION for your family. You could
choose a special occasion, or any
everyday opportunity, to shape an
EPIC MOMENT. Be as specific and
inspired as possible!

_____

_____

_____

_____

_____

_____

_____

_____

_____

_____

_____

_____

_____

_____

_____

Loving Kindness

right speech + right action

Loving kindness is coming to the sacred party this week—just in time for winter gatherings of family and friends. We invite you to take up a LOVING-KINDNESS PRACTICE *by becoming more aware of how you speak and move through the world. Noticing this lets you strengthen your "kindness muscles," and gives your child the gifts of peace, serenity, and compassion. As lofty as those goals may sound, they are certainly worth pursuing, and the daily workout will have you spiritually fit in no time!*

YOU ⚬⌁

Being kind makes you kinda rad! But what if you could be loving *and* kind? Then you could really strut your stuff. No doubt, some days you are *all that*—and more. But other days are just plain crappy.

That's okay—loving kindness is a PRACTICE. Even the most peace-filled monks in the world will tell you that they must practice this concept everyday. And of course, like any practice, the more you do it the better you get, and the easier it becomes.

If you want to embrace the practice of loving kindness, then you can get right to work on the sacred intention for RIGHT SPEECH and RIGHT ACTION. This may sound easy, but it can be really hard to implement at every turn, especially in the chaos of motherhood. When you say YES to right speech, you take time with your words, and start to fall in love with new ways to speak hard truths. And, when you say YES to right action, your heart is open to actions that only transmit love, and you live with integrity by walking your talk.

When you say YES to both, you become a student of loving kindness, and plenty of opportunities to practice will come your way. This means that when your buttons get pushed, you might see it as a gift to help you cultivate your loving kindness.

YOUR SOUL ⟡

When words are both true and kind, they can change the world.
—THE BUDDHA

It's easy for most of us to stay loving when everything is peachy in our lives. The challenging part is staying loving when things go to shit. This is the realm of PRACTICE! And this is where the opportunity to grow arises within each of us. Can you be kind when someone is unkind to you? Can you recognize that it is more important to be kind than to be right?

When put to the test, your soul will answer with kindness, as souls tend to do. But the mind can interrupt right action with chatter about fairness and righteousness. As a mother, it is always better to follow your soul's lead and take the high road. In the end, you will feel better and be able to make way for spiritual growth. Surrendering the need to be right requires you to be egoless, and when you shed ego, you start down your path to *nirvana*.

YOUR CHILD ⟡

Children are born kind. As pure, loving spirits, they know no other way. But as they grow, they learn from those around them. What are you teaching your children? Every day, they need to hear your loving words in order to shape their own. And they need your right action to help them know how to live.

Your children need you to be noble, like a benevolent queen, because you have their hearts in your hands. You must handle that responsibility with the utmost of care. What you say and how you act matters to your children—they see and hear everything! While you cannot be perfect, you can rise to the challenge of being noble. This is worth striving for, with fierce love. Teach your child by your right speech and your right action; it will be the best education they can ever receive.

REFLECTIONS ◌

There is no way to happiness. Happiness is the way.
—THICH NHAT HANH

In this moment, see where you land on the true-happiness scale. Do you feel you generally live in loving kindness, or do you hang out at the other end of the spectrum, in anger and fear? How would you prefer to act and feel?

Who were your role models as you were growing up? Was loving kindness the mantra of the day when you were a child? Take some time to reflect, and take stock. Try not to pass any judgment—just notice your memories and your feelings. Awareness is the first step to walking your own heart path, because it empowers you with choice.

SACRED MOTHERHOOD PRACTICES ◌

TAKE UP THE KINDNESS WORKOUT. Every morning, before life gets crazy busy, take five minutes to meditate on stepping into the highest vibration you can muster. Pick one kind word to use as your mantra throughout the day. You can use an inspirational deck to help guide this reminder of right speech and right action, or you can just come up with a word on your own. You will be amazed by how this simple act can help shift your energy. Training your mind to work with kind words is a great way to start this *sacred* workout.

IDEAS ◌

- BRING SMILING TO YOUR CONSCIOUS AWARENESS. Practice smiling throughout the day. Whenever you feel your vibration lowering, SMILE! This practice raises you up and helps remind you that you are full of love and joy. You can also uplift another person by smiling at them, which tells you that smiling is part of RIGHT ACTION.

- BREW IT! MAKE SOME LOVING-KINDNESS TEA. When your family needs to be infused with a little loving kindness, brew up some of this tea.

LOVING-KINDNESS TEA

(compliments of Jessica Booth from Sacred Essence)

1 cup dried chamomile flowers

1 cup dried lavender flowers

½ cup dried organic rose petals

½ cup dried elderflowers

optional: 1 cup loose green tea

Mix the herbs together, and steep 2–3 spoonsful in a cup of freshly boiled water for five minutes. Then enjoy!

pairings ☙

- Book: *How to Love* by Thich Nhat Hanh

- Crystal: Peridot is a gentle-natured "happy stone" that brings healing to your heart chakra and balance to your emotional life. It also supports you in loving yourself when you make mistakes. Consider making or buying a peridot mala (prayer-bead string) to help keep you in a state of loving kindness to yourself and others.

journal on

Loving Kindness

Write about what right action and right speech mean to you as a mother. Where are you golden regarding these, and where could your loving-kindness practice benefit from a little more intention? Finally, jot down some loving and kind words that you can add to your daily kindness workout.

Breaking Bread

homemade traditions

In the winter months, when hearth and home mean everything, breaking bread with others can be an essential part of sharing seasonal fun and friendship. "Breaking bread" can literally mean sharing a loaf of bread with others. Or it can serve as a metaphor for having a meal together. Either way, BREAKING BREAD *is all about strengthening communal and family ties through* HOMEMADE FOOD AND TRADITIONS.

YOU ⌾⌾

Breaking bread is a *sacred* act. When you break bread with others, you share more than food; you share a piece of your soul, your essence, and your commitment to the tribe. The bread is the medium, passed from hand to hand, that carries the spirit of connecting in a meaningful way. Think about what breaking bread means to *you*—whom do you want at your table to share in this communal way?

Being a part of the greater circle of community in a thoughtful and wholehearted way brings a richer purpose to life, and can so easily teach our children about caring for and connecting with others. I love the old image of a table full of monks who only ate with very long chopsticks, so that they could only feed the person across the table, rather than themselves. Food builds community! So as you light your hearth-fire this season, consider inviting others to break bread with your family, and reap the many rewards of generosity and *tribe.*

YOUR SOUL ⌾⌾

You are the boss of that dough.
—JULIA CHILD

Bread is a symbol as well as a sustainer of life. It contains the heart and soul of whoever makes it, and it absolutely can nourish the mind, body, and spirit. Bread makes you work for her splendor, and pushes you to pay close attention along the way to her glory. It's a journey and a meditation that results in lasting memories. The smell of baking bread is a lingering sensory experience, and taps into the very meaning of comfort and home.

If you take up bread-baking as a practice, invite your conscious awareness to the party and bake all of your love into every loaf. Then bring the concept of BREAKING BREAD to any sacred, special meal you hold in your home: Pass around a loaf of your homemade bread. Ask everyone to tear off a piece, then eat the pieces at the same time as a blessing of gratitude for the shared LOVE in the room.

YOUR CHILD ⌐∿

Every home needs traditions and ceremonies that enhance the sacred experience of life. When I started my own family, I knew I wanted to mark transitional times of the year and life in special, meaningful ways that our children would remember and maybe pass down to their children. I was always a bit envious of folks around me who had special food traditions that I didn't. Luckily, the beauty of motherhood is that we get to write whatever story we want for our families. We can choose to keep ancient traditions alive, or we can create new ones to enliven our evolving beliefs.

One day, my husband and I decided that we would make all of our own bread for one year. This seemed daunting at first, but we came to really enjoy making bread every Sunday evening—and our kids loved it too! We have made all kinds of bread since we started this tradition, and our kids have learned that there is something really sacred about baking and breaking bread with loved ones.

Fresh bread also makes great gifts! As an added blessing, there is just something about playing with bread dough that makes kids happy. Dough is great to have on hand for snowy days and family dinner parties. It's fun, and keeps little hands occupied for longer than a minute!

REFLECTIONS ⌐∿

As humans, we are meant to live in harmonious community with others, not isolated in boxy homes. *We need each other!* Look within to see how you feel about being a part of community and opening your home and hearth to others. Is your home a place that people naturally gravitate toward, seeking solace and friendship—or are your doors, energetically speaking, kept closed? How can you bring both your biological and chosen families together around an inspired vision of recreating TRIBE?

SACRED MOTHERHOOD PRACTICE ❧

PRACTICE BREAD THERAPY. Consciously bake bread, with love and intention, once a week for a whole month. This is a simple practice, and should include the whole family. Try saying a prayer at the beginning to set your intention, play bread-making music (see "Pairings" below), and laugh into the dough. You want to infuse the bread with your love and high vibrations. At the end, share the bread with each other, and perhaps make extra to share with a neighbor or send off to school for a teacher.

IDEAS ❧

- BAKE BREAD! Here is a great recipe for a traditional braided bread that is easy to make, tastes great, and will bring high-vibe energy to any BREAKING-BREAD celebration.

BASIC HOMEMADE BREAD

2 cups hot water

2 tablespoons dry active yeast

⅓ cup sugar

2 teaspoons salt

⅓ cup vegetable oil

½ teaspoon garlic powder

½ teaspoon dried oregano

4–5 cups flour, plus a little extra

Mix the first seven ingredients together, then add two cups of flour and mix well for 2 minutes. Slowly add in the remaining flour, until dough forms a ball. Set it on a floured surface, and knead in more flour until the dough is no longer sticky.

Place dough in an oiled bowl to rise for 1 hour. Split the dough in half, then separate each half into three small balls. Roll each small ball into a rope about one inch thick and the length of a bread loaf; then place on an oiled cookie sheet and braid the three strands together.

Let rise for 30 minutes. Bake at 375° for 15–20 minutes.

· GIFT IT. Pick a day during the holidays to bake a few varieties of bread with your children. Once the loaves are baked, wrap them up and deliver them to homeless shelters, soup kitchens, or folks on the street who need food. This act of generosity and love teaches your children about gratitude and loving their larger community.

· HOLD A COMMUNITY STONE SOUP GATHERING. The story of Stone Soup is that one person (*you!*) can bring a whole community together by starting a soup with nothing but water and plain stones. Guests arrive to add other yummy ingredients, plus their love. And then *all* share the incredible soup together as a community, along with some homemade bread! Here is a recipe to get you started.

STONE SOUP

Makes 4 servings. Double, triple, or quadruple to feed your whole TRIBE!

    3 palm-size stones, thoroughly cleaned

    1 tablespoon unsalted butter

    1 yellow onion, diced

    3 garlic cloves, minced

    2 quarts vegetable stock, homemade or purchased

    2 chicken bouillon cubes

3 cups water

2 zucchinis, chopped into child-size bites

3 tomatoes, chopped

3 carrots, chopped

3 pieces of celery, chopped

1½ cups green beans, chopped

Sea salt and pepper, to taste

In a soup pot, melt the butter and add onions and garlic. Sauté for about 6 minutes. Add vegetable stock, bouillon cubes, water and stones. Add in zucchinis, tomatoes, carrots, celery, and green beans. Season with sea salt and pepper.

Simmer on low heat for approximately 30 minutes, or until vegetables are cooked through. Remove the stones—do not serve them! But set them aside, as kids like to have them afterward. With your homemade bread, this makes a warm and hearty meal!

pairings ✑

- Children's book: *Stone Soup* by Marcia Brown
- Music: Anything by Edith Piaf, a Parisian singer whose voice and songs create the ambiance of a French bistro—complete with a baguette, a bottle of good wine, and beloved friends.

Breaking Bread

List the names of friends and family who you want to nourish with your love, food, and good vibes. Plan a menu, set a date, and draft the invitation. Then commit to making this warm and welcoming communal gathering *happen!*

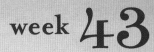

Family

we are one and many

The word "family" has many definitions. The unity and safety of your nuclear family is familiar territory, but you can expand your range of relations to include a TRIBE of chosen family as well. Your assorted familial roots don't define you, but they do shape you, and can be amazing touchstones for your identity. This week, as you curl up in a nest of loved ones by the fire, take time to look more closely at your own family—how you define it, breathe life into it, and ultimately experience connection.

YOU ☙

Give the ones you love wings to fly, roots to come back to, and reasons to stay.
—THE DALAI LAMA

Before starting a family of your own, your definition of family probably defaulted to the one you grew up in, for better or for worse. Your childhood family experience is a part of your dharmic path. As such, it was a hotbed of life lessons for you—how to love, and be loved; how to express yourself, and receive what others have to share; how to meet your needs alongside those of others; and how to be kind and compassionate. This wisdom can be hard-won even in the happiest, warm-fuzziest families.

As you begin your own family, ideally you have been blessed with the unconditional love and support of your parents and siblings, and can look forward to recreating aspects of your original family as you shape your own. Yet your own little family is a beautiful, never-before-seen creation. You are blending both your and your beloved's backgrounds, and you are calling in new ways to support authenticity and awareness as you manifest your own SACRED FAMILY.

Just as your parents do not control the life you are creating, ultimately you cannot direct your children's lives either. You can, however, create a strong and caring family to offer your children deep roots and a safety net, to help keep them grounded and supported no matter what they do or where they are in the world. The consciousness you bring to laying a loving foundation and creating healthy family dynamics will help your babies experience both freedom *and* connection when they leave the nest and fly off to form their own TRIBE.

YOUR SOUL ☙

Who would you say is a part of your TRIBE? Were you born into a family that feeds you deeply? Or is your family not especially resonant with you or your purpose in the world? Either way, you need to nurture deep relations with others who speak your language. These chosen relations form your SOUL FAMILY. They are the people who just *get* you, and support you in your spiritual growth.

As a mama you especially need a *person*—one special someone—who is always, in all ways, there for you. This person is family, blood-related or not, and is someone you can confide in who will be there to hold you when you fall. This could be your partner in life, your mom, an aunt, or a soul-sister. Who in your life shows up for you in this way?

YOUR CHILD ☙

Our family is just one tent away from a full-blown circus.
—UNKNOWN

"Family" for us equates with wild, chaotic fun. Some days, when all four of my kids are on my bed wrestling, giggling, talking over each other, and trying to middle-grab some snuggle time with me, I think to myself, "This is all there is!" It is my circus, and there is no greater joy than what I experience in those moments. Family is the fabric of our lives, sewn together by the beauty of simple, real, love-rich moments.

Your children need to understand their place in the patchwork of your family quilt—how they are seen and loved, what they have to offer, and how they are uniquely designed to fit perfectly within *your* family. It can be helpful to take note of birth order in your family. In Waldorf philosophy, it is said that the first child is the *thinker,* the second child is the *feeler,* and the third child the *doer.* How might this idea shine light on the dynamics of the children in your family?

REFLECTIONS ⚜

What was family life like when you were growing up? Can you remember special moments that leave a twinkle in your eye? Were there hard times that still burden you? We all have family wounds. The best we can do is to work on healing them so that we can do better with our own families. What are some of the ways you would like to reshape the definition of family in your home now?

SACRED MOTHERHOOD PRACTICE ⚜

CREATE I SEE YOU PRAYER FLAGS. Using 5 x 7-inch pieces of muslin or other cotton fabric, make a prayer flag for each person in your family, and write his or her name on it. Pass each loved one's flag around to the other family members, along with fabric pens, and invite them to write or draw something they especially love or appreciate about that person. You may want to add a few flags of prayers for your family as a whole, or make flags for "soul-family" members who do not live in your home. Once the flags are finished, share the blessings and the I SEE YOU reflections out loud. Then sew or clothespin them onto a cord, and hang them up in your sacred home!

IDEAS ⚜

- CREATE A FAMILY DREAM BOX. Invite each person to contribute ideas for family nature adventures, local excursions, museum visits, and so on. Write down all of the dreams on slips of paper and put them into a special dream box that you decorate together. One at a time, pull out a dream to manifest with your whole family.

- PLAN A WINTER GETAWAY WITH A GROUP OF FAMILIES. Escape to a child-friendly hot springs, a snowbound winter hut, or even the nearest beach. Be sure there is plenty of opportunity for downtime, multigenerational fun, and group meals, and you will have the essential ingredients for creating your TRIBE.

pAiRiNgs ⌒

- Children's book: *The Invisible String* by Patrice Karst
- Music: "We Are Family" by Sister Sledge

journal on

Family

Spend time reflecting on both your
blood family and your soul family.
What does "family" mean to you?
Have you found your go-to person?
Have you found your TRIBE?

Sisterhood

finding your tribe

As winter wears on, the isolating chill and gloom drives home the importance of belonging to a TRIBE. *It is a time to share our light, our warmth, our food, and our love. Even in a tropical paradise, at some point motherhood manifests as that longest, darkest night when we realize that we cannot survive alone. Sisters, heed the wise words of a Hopi elder: "The time for the lone wolf is over. Gather yourselves!"*

YOU ℮∿

Now is the time to take a tribal inventory: Who are your people? Whom can you call upon when fever strikes, and you can't leave the house to gather ingredients for the requisite chicken soup? Whom can you lean on when you feel afraid or disheartened? Which sisters can you gather to celebrate and *howl at the moon?*

If these questions give you pause, it is likely that motherhood has brought about a need for some tribal reorganization. Maybe mothering has dispersed the circles that supported you in maidenhood. Quite possibly, work and home life have captured all of your time, leaving you without idle hours for entering deep space with a dear friend. Or perhaps you find yourself anchored in a new community through playdates and carpools, and feel called to further cultivate those connections.

No matter where you stand in the social spectrum, sisterhood is a salve that all mothers should have at their fingertips. What can you do this week to rally your tribe of TRUE SISTERS?

YOUR SOUL ℮∿

What is sisterhood? In short, it is everything—inspiration, love, good food, cranky vibes, joy, flowers, empowerment, creativity, bliss, tears, belly laughs, honesty, blood, and beauty. Sisterhood is where our feminine power and grace is mirrored. By the time we become mothers, the days of petty friendships and catty competitions are over. Motherhood demands authenticity, and honoring of self and others.

Imagine a sisterhood where each woman is celebrated for her unique gifts, supported in her most vulnerable moments, and encouraged to manifest her grandest vision. As these women sit in circle together, a potent field of strength and presence is created, and radiates outward to benefit the entire community. If this describes your tribe, REJOICE! If not, take heart; this reality is closer than you may imagine.

Every woman holds the seed of this desire and potential; you simply need to open a safe space in which it can germinate. Whether you reconvene a group of old friends, or take steps to start a new Sacred Motherhood Circle, make sisterhood a priority this week. Then watch how the ripples renew your soul and refresh your mothering energy.

YOUR CHILD ☙

Not only is tribe essential for your well-being, it creates a garden of comfort and stability in which your whole family will thrive. Within an extended circle of trusted aunties, uncles, and cousins, your children can feel welcomed and seen. They come to know that they can turn to others when they are in need of help, and that they too can contribute their hearts and hands to the community. This web of mutual support also takes some of the pressure off of you, while modeling for your children how to work together to meet everyone's needs and laying the foundation for living in cooperation and compassion later in their lives.

REFLECTIONS ☙

If sisterhood eludes you, ask yourself why you are a lone wolf. It is okay to want to spend time alone—but if you find that you're isolating yourself, consider whether past wounds or unconscious beliefs may be contributing to your aloneness. Were you forever disillusioned by junior-high cliques? Has mainstream American culture inclined you toward independence rather than interdependence? Whatever the reason, get to the bottom of your tendency to keep to yourself, and give sisterhood another try. Motherhood offers an opportunity to create lifelong friends for both you and your family—and this is the season for gathering together.

SACRED MOTHERHOOD PRACTICE ❧

MAKE AN OFFERING IN THE NAME OF SISTERHOOD. Brighten a friend's winter day with some flowers and a heartfelt note. Drop off dinner to someone in your community who could use a break. And you know that woman you pass anonymously each day? Greet her warmly, and introduce yourself. You never know where a sister is waiting to be found.

IDEAS ❧

- CREATE A SACRED MOTHERHOOD CIRCLE. Invite a few friends, along with a couple of other chosen mama acquaintances, to a mothers' gathering. Use this book to help you create an altar, identify prompts to invite contribution, and get underway. Or sign up for one of our Sacred Motherhood Retreats and learn to lead a year-long circle, following the rhythm of the seasons to seed inspiration, intention, and sisterhood into the soul of motherhood. (Check our website for more details: www.sacred-motherhood.com.)

- INVEST IN THE BARTER ECONOMY OF MOTHERHOOD. With another mama or two, set up a childcare trade so that you can make it to yoga class once a week. Or take turns working in each others' yards to create the gardens of your dreams. Passing along baby gear and outgrown clothes to families in your community is another great way to forge friendships.

PAIRINGS ❧

- Sacred Living Movement Retreats: Sacred Motherhood and I AM Sisterhood
- Music: "Crazy Beautiful" by Skylar Stecker
- Training (not Sacred Living Movement): Women's Temple Group Leadership Training by Awakening Women (www.awakening women.com)

journal on

Sisterhood

Describe your most dreamy vision
of true sisterhood: What does it
look like? Where does it happen?
How does it feel? Who might be
able to join you in making your
dream a reality? Now *make it happen!*

Connection

a bond like no other

A cozy fire on a wintry evening offers up the perfect opportunity to snuggle with your dear ones. In this mood of hibernation, it is easy to foster the deep connections that nourish family ties and nurture individual well-being. Allow yourself to relax into the seasonal nest, and reflect on the bond you share with your children— A BOND LIKE NO OTHER.

YOU ♐

Our bond with our children is unique. We are honored to serve as vessels for their bodies during pregnancy, and then learn to best support them as they grow along their own paths in life. The sweet intimacy we share when they are small and mama-centric changes over time. Though we are always deeply connected, the push and pull of this ever-changing relationship influences the quality of mother-child dynamics as well. At times you will be totally in synch—then, out of the blue, you may feel you are living with a stranger.

The best you can do, as a tenderhearted, fully human mama, is to tune in and just roll with it. Be kind to yourself, as you notice that one minute you are relaxed and available to connect—but the next you are frazzled and disengaged. Try not to take it personally if one day your child can't get enough of your love—but the next they are embarrassed to kiss you goodbye.

Through it all, create spaces in your day and week when you spend time together, no matter what. Open your lap to your child after school every afternoon, and listen to whatever they have to share. Or steal a quiet, candlelit moment as your child drifts off to sleep each night. Find what works for you, and then make the commitment to be totally present.

YOUR SOUL ♐

Any connection you share with your children begins with a deep connection to *yourself.* Take a moment to close your eyes and quiet your mind. Notice your breath, and then bring your awareness into your body—your belly, face, shoulders, hands, and feet. What feelings or sensations are arising for you in this moment? Do you feel tension, ease, warmth, or discomfort? Breathe into whatever is present, and inquire into what might be underlying your physical experience. Are you anxious about a work project? Have you been staying up too late at night? Do you have cabin-fever?

This practice is especially helpful when you are having difficulty connecting with your children. Like all mothers, you probably experience moments when you feel yourself contracting. Sometimes you might not be aware that you have descended into this state; maybe you just feel irritated or distracted. If, however, you pause and take a few breaths while scanning your body, you may discover tightness in your belly, or notice that you are holding your shoulders up to your ears. As you feel this tension, some sadness, disappointment, or resentment may surface. Just stay with the feeling, and have compassion for yourself. Often, just bringing awareness to a feeling allows it to move along, making room again for real, gratifying connection with ourselves and others too.

YOUR CHILD ⌒

Your young child lives in a world of ONENESS with the family, and especially with you, as you hold the center. "Attachment parenting" nurtures this tender worldview with practices such as breastfeeding, baby-wearing, and co-sleeping, all of which strengthen the bond between mother and child.

The gifts of this approach are priceless and enduring. Any child thrives in a world in which SAFETY, TRUST, and LOVE are their ground of being. And you may soften your heart and soothe old wounds as you bask in your little one's purity and innocence. Years later, in the throes of adolescence or the heartbreak of an empty nest, both of you may return to this core connection and find solace.

REFLECTIONS ⌒

Though divine love surrounds us and is available in every moment, we are cursed with amnesia, and often forget that we exist in the embrace of GRACE. Our Earthly existence is an experiment in the perceived separateness that begins the moment we physically disconnect from our mother's womb. Perhaps we are all trying to find our way back into the lap of oneness through our connections with others. If we entertain the idea that we are already *whole and held,* how might we act differently in our relationships?

SACRED MOTHERHOOD PRACTICE ⤳

FOSTER CONNECTION. This week, experiment with finding the perfect time and place to connect with your children, and then have fun making it a sacred practice. If you decide to offer foot rubs before bed each night, buy some yummy lavender lotion. Or if you designate Sunday morning as the holy moment to stay in bed and snuggle as a family, be sure to have enough pillows on hand to welcome all the sleepy heads.

IDEAS ⤳

- TURN TO THE CARDS. Pull out *The Mother's Wisdom Deck* or any favorite inspirational cards. Set the intention to choose cards that will illuminate your connection to your children. Draw one card for each child, and then take time to consider how they might reflect both the shining moments and the shadow moments in your relationship with them.

- TAKE YOUR CHILD ON A DATE. Chose something out of the ordinary that you and your child would both enjoy. Make arrangements so that it can be just the two of you. And be sure to turn off your cell phone!

- PRACTICE INTENTIONAL EYE GAZING WITH YOUR CHILD. Place your hand on your child's heart and intentionally stare into her eyes while playing "Sacred Perfect" by Nina Lee. Send your child ALL your love for the duration of the song.

PAIRINGS ⤳

- Sacred Living Moment Retreat: Sacred Beginnings (online)
- Music: "Child and Mother" by Nina Lee

Connection

What do you cherish most about the connection between you and your child? Highlight a few beautiful and memorable moments in your relationship. Then ask: When have you felt disconnected, and why? What is one thing you could do to strengthen your connection?

Superpowers

rise up, wonder woman!

I'm not saying I'm Wonder Woman, but nobody has ever seen us in the same room! Just sayin'.
—UNKNOWN

As the winter months begin to test your strength and endurance, it can be helpful to look within, and see how powerful and amazing you truly are. Mothers have many superpowers that we don't see as extraordinary, but they are—and you are! This week, we'll get to know your WONDER WOMAN *side, revealing the mysterious and bad-ass superhero that lives within you.*

YOU ⌇

Always wear your invisible crown.
—UNKNOWN

First of all, you are a mother and a woman. By virtue of this fact alone, you are bad-ass! Mothers *can* do it all—not that you *should* do it all, but you surely can. Weeks float by without a nod to the amount you accomplish every day as you feed children, work, clean up, create, play, and nurture without even blinking. As a mother, you are likely to find yourself responding to an email while answering kids' questions, while finding some lost treasured item, while hugging and kissing someone who needs you in that moment, *and* while cooking dinner—all at the same time—while planning the rest of the evening in your head.

These are the superpowers all mothers are blessed with, from the first moment they hold their babies and life begins anew. The wee problem with this is that sometimes, without even noticing, you can give away your life-force as you use your superpowers in daily actions. This in turn can lead to exhaustion and a feeling of overwhelm. Here's the good news: You possess a special superpower—one that *only* you have. It was given to you on the day you came into this life, and is your defining WONDER. This magical quality is what makes you the unique person that you are. It is your spark and your shine in the world. Your inner WONDER WOMAN wants to rise-up and be *seen.* She wants you to claim her! Once you do that, there is no stopping the marvel that you are.

YOUR SOUL ⌘

What does it mean to honor the WONDER WOMAN within? First, remember that you are a WOMAN before anything else; you vibrate with the rhythms of moon and ocean and other elemental superpowers as naturally as you breathe the air. With the primordial heartbeat of Mother Earth within your chest, and fire in your belly, you can be compassionate and passionate in the same breath. Can you put even *more* wonder in your womanhood? Try owning *this.*

You are BRAVE—take hold of your life as an adventure. You are STRONG—take risks for the greater good. You are KIND—take care of yourself with the same loving generosity you freely give the world. You are ONE with the universe—take up your sword of wisdom to guide and protect your children and all children. You *are* all these kinds of wonderful. All you have to do is believe it, and be it.

YOUR CHILD ⌘

Children believe in magic, fairies, moon dust, and superheroes. They believe that they are invincible! Where do all those beliefs float off to, when we grow up? Sometimes the dose of reality we dole out to children is a little too much, and the magic that is so real to them gets pushed to the side.

Encourage your children to stand smack-dab in the middle of their sparkly world, and dance and twirl in it. Children don't need to see to believe—*they believe, and therefore they can see.* Allowing them to live in this extraordinary world as long as possible is a way to honor their grandest visions for life and for themselves.

REFLECTIONS ⌘

When a woman transitions into motherhood, she loses something but gains much. Her maidenhood is no longer, but she is WOMAN;

she is mother. And she has the special wisdom that only motherhood can offer.

In this culture, however, motherhood doesn't always receive the accolades it deserves. It's so important to *claim your own power* as a mother, so that you can shine as your brightest self. How do you *truly* feel about being a mom? Do you feel like a bad-ass Wonder Woman? Or do you feel you are drowning in kid duties, and have a hard time keeping up? Notice your feelings, reflect on them, and understand that while you are capable of doing *anything*, you are the one who must activate your superpowers!

SACRED MOTHERHOOD PRACTICE ◌◌

TAKE SUPERHERO SELFIES. Take pictures of yourself, so you can see your light shine forth. It's important to look closely at these self-portraits, so that you can see your own beauty and superpowers growing and reshaping over time. Take this a step further: When you wake up every day, remind yourself that you are the WONDER WOMAN of your family, pledged to practice your superpowers for the good of all!

IDEAS ◌◌

- CLAIM YOUR SUPERPOWER! Stand tall, with feet apart, hands on hips, and head held high. Announce to the universe what your superpower is. Claim it! Yell it three times, to make it ring loud and true in your heart. Then live your life with the knowing that you possess a secret superpower that nobody else in the world has quite like you do.

- SHINE YOUR LIGHT! Create your own Shine-Your-Light Oil to remind you that you are a bad-ass Wonder Woman!

SHINE-YOUR-LIGHT OIL

(A gift from the Sacred Essence program)

10 drops palo santo essential oil

3 drops "Bird of Paradise" essence from Soul Tree Essences
(available from www.thejessrose.com, and www.mamababywise
.co.uk)

Fill a ⅓-ounce rollertop bottle nearly full with Rose Oil (see
"Ideas" in Week 2) and add the above ingredients. Wear this oil
every day.

pairings ☙

- Crystal: Tiger's eye is a wonder stone to use for sharpening the
  senses and amping up the motherhood superpowers of strength,
  confidence, and bravery.
- Music: "Rise Up" by Andra Day; "Run the World (Girls)" by
  Beyoncé; "I Know Who I Am" by Leona Lewis; "A Little Bit
  Stronger" by Leighton Meester; "Roar" by Katy Perry; and "Fight
  Song" by Rachel Platten

Superpowers

Take some time to meditate on what your secret SUPERPOWER is, what it means to you, and how you can use it for the good of your family and the world! Write about it here.

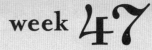

Speaking + Listening

from the heart

Imagine a world where the only words spoken are KIND WORDS. *And what if* DEEP LISTENING *were a centerpiece of all relationships? The way we speak and listen to one another is at the heart of everything—family, marriage, friendship, politics, war, and peace. 'Tis the season to gather with friends and family, and pray for peace on Earth. What better time to mind and mend the ways of our words?*

YOU ⟡〜

With motherhood comes the realization that words are powerful. Some phrases we speak work like a charm. Others wreak havoc on tender souls. While you no doubt strive to use only the most caring and compassionate speech with your children, you have also probably yelled at them, or said something you wish you hadn't. Motherhood brings out the best and the worst in all of us!

In this way, motherhood again calls you to your growing edge. It asks you to do the hard work of acknowledging where your words are not kind or honest or validating of others. You can then make amends, and try again. If certain situations tend to pull you back into bad habits, you may find it helpful to prepare a couple of well-crafted sentences to keep at the ready. Here are few to try with young children that were inspired by beloved Waldorf teachers:

- When your child is shouting or yelling indoors, you could suggest, "Let's go open the door and put our big voice outside, then bring our inside voice back with us."

- When your child ignores your direction, you can say, "Let's have a seat and grow our listening ears."

- When a child has said something unkind, you might respond with "We shall polish our hearts and use our golden words."

YOUR SOUL ⟡〜

How can you express yourself clearly if you are lost in the chatter of your "monkey mind" and disconnected from your inner truth? Especially in situations where you feel overwhelmed or befuddled, take time to cut through the muddling layers *before* you open your mouth. This can be as simple as breathing deeply before making a request of your child. Or it might be a more involved process when delving into mucky waters with a loved one.

Try grabbing your journal and writing through your reactions and feelings until you arrive at the *heart* of the matter. From this grounded place, you will be able to better express yourself with LOVE and AUTHENTICITY.

YOUR CHILD ☙

Have you ever heard your child say something unbecoming that made you cringe? You'd like to think that they picked it up from someone at school—but you have to admit that they sound just like—who? You guessed it—*you!*

Children are master imitators, so our speech must not only be kind and honest, it must be *worthy* of imitation. Luckily, there is nothing like your children parroting your worst habits to motivate speech reform!

Don't stop at simply eliminating potty talk. Work to really understand how you communicate: Do you talk too much or too fast? Do you refrain from saying what is really in your heart? Do you have a habit of interrupting? Once you have a clearer picture of what you'd like to change, turn your attention to modeling good communication. Let your children hear you share your feelings, make clear requests, work out differences, apologize, admit mistakes, and express gratitude, joy, and appreciation. This is how they will learn right speech from you.

REFLECTIONS ☙

"Communication" came from the Latin word *communicare*, "to share." Yet we can talk a blue streak and never actually say anything meaningful. Similarly, when we do not truly listen to others, we easily misunderstand what they are trying to say. Your children respond better to fewer words, and blossom when they feel heard. Let them be your *greatest teachers* when it comes to speaking and listening from the heart.

SACRED MOTHERHOOD PRACTICE ⌒

CREATE A FAMILY COUNCIL. Once a week, or once a month, sit in a circle, light a candle, and offer a dedication. Pass around a talking piece—a special rock or stick that you have decorated together— and practice the art of speaking and listening from the heart. The person holding the talking piece is the only one who speaks, keeping their words authentic, spontaneous, and simple. The others listen without judgment or comment. You can pick a theme for the council, or leave it open to whatever is arising for each person in that moment.

IDEAS ⌒

- ORGANIZE OR ATTEND A NONVIOLENT COMMUNICATION (NVC) WORKSHOP. Founded by Marshall Rosenberg, NVC is a tool for expressing feelings, needs, and requests without blaming or withdrawing. A local NVC organization can put you in touch with a facilitator. (Visit www.cnvc.org for more information and resources.)

- CREATE A BOOK OF PHRASES. Begin writing down phrases that you can use with your children in situations most likely to trigger your negative reactions. Think about what you truly want to communicate at these times, and how your words can be both kind and direct.

PAIRINGS ⌒

- Books: *The Way of Council* by Virginia Coyle and Jack Zimmerman and *Parenting From Your Heart: Sharing the Gifts of Compassion, Connection, and Choice* by Inbal Kashtan

journal on

Speaking + Listening

Recall a recent conversation when you didn't feel heard. Describe the situation and the feelings it stirred. What core need or desire (such as intimacy, respect, or acceptance) were you hoping to fulfill? How did you express this desire? How do you think it was heard? If it wasn't heard and fulfilled, how might you express that need differently in the future?

Discipline

following the inner guide

The teachings of the Medicine Wheel, which inspired the seasonal arrangement of this book, pair winter with structures that help individuals thrive and serve the greater good. This week, we shine a light on discipline, a scaffold that buttresses your family's well-being. Discipline is forever a work in progress, so set aside expectations of mastery. Instead, focus on the unseen forces that can either topple or strengthen your approach to this multidimensional art.

YOU ⌾⁀

Discipline is one of the most challenging responsibilities of mother-hood. It is impossible to always see the bigger picture and say the right thing. It is harder still not to take it personally or come undone when your child misbehaves. Like every other mother, you will fall down in this effort. Perhaps you will utter shaming words, or dole out an irra-tional consequence. What then? Pick yourself up, and BE KIND—not only to your child but also to yourself.

Discipline is a complex topic. Volumes have been written on the subject, yet every mother must come to terms with her own process and approach. There are many forces at play; if you are conscious of them, you'll be better able to navigate rough waters.

Start by recalling how you were disciplined as a child. How does this influence your mothering, for better or worse? Next, reflect on your partner's disciplinary approach. Are the two of you aligned, complementary, or at odds? Most importantly, consider your chil-dren. Are they free spirits, or rule-followers? When do they need boundaries to thrive? Where can you encourage their sovereignty?

As you ponder these questions, bear in mind that there is no magic formula. What works for one child may not work for a child of a different temperament. Likewise, what feels solid to you may feel shaky to another mama. What to do? FOLLOW YOUR INNER GUIDE.

YOUR SOUL ⌾⁀

How do you find that inner guide? First, be wary of imposters. When your child challenges you, your ego may swoop in and assert her false will. Your reaction is likely to sound controlling and righteous. You'll be quick to say things like, "Because I said so" and "Because I know best," in an attempt to keep everything under wraps. Sound familiar?

Perhaps you're also acquainted with your superego, the inner voice that works diligently to keep you on track by criticizing, nagging, and worrying you. She sounds a bit like a neurotic mother, right? Like a mother, your superego means well; she wants you to be safe and successful. But when she oversteps her bounds and tries to tell you how to parent, simply say, "Thank you. I'm okay, and will no longer be needing your services."

Once you've acknowledged and quieted the broken records, you can tune into the guidance of your internal Wise Woman—the inner voice arising from your *essence*. You can trust her to discern what is in balance, appropriate, and in the flow. She will help you take right action, and find the right words. She knows when to heed good advice, and when to come back to her own truth. And, she works to ensure your safety and the safety of others from a space of deep WISDOM and TRUST rather than control and fear.

YOUR CHILD ⌒

Helping your children develop and trust their own sound inner guidance is the intention of Sacred Discipline. It honors children's *inherent goodness* while holding space for the whole gamut of behaviors that may surface as children grow and individuate. When you maintain the perspective that children truly want to experience and express their highest selves, it is easier to hear misbehaviors as cries for help rather than reacting to them as a personal affront.

Like all of us, your children will have a hard time being at their best when they feel stressed by pressures or changes in life. Acting out is a sign that they feel off, and cannot find the terra firma within themselves. They are asking you to bring in age-appropriate reinforcements. Enter Sacred Discipline—the establishing of firm but kind boundaries and guidance to support children as they orient themselves in the world and fine-tune their internal compasses.

REFLECTIONS ❧

The dance of discipline will keep you on your toes. It is an exercise in compassion, and a call to exorcise your own demons. When you run into challenges, chances are you've encountered a behavior that triggers a reaction rather than a response. Before you can respond calmly and clearly to your child, you'll need to reconcile your reaction. This is your soul's work on the sacred path of motherhood.

SACRED MOTHERHOOD PRACTICE ❧

PRACTICE BEING PRESENT. Many disciplinary challenges simply fall away when you step into your child's day with your grounded presence. Give each child your undivided attention for ten minutes in the morning, twenty minutes during the day, and another ten minutes in the evening. Inspire your partner to do the same.

IDEAS ❧

- FOLLOW THE RULE OF TENS. Commit to taking a deep breath and counting to ten before disciplining your child. This gives you time to call in your inner Wise Woman before you speak or act. Grant your children the same leeway. After making a request, count to ten before expecting them to respond.

- COMPARE NOTES. Sit down with your partner, and have a conversation about discipline. Identify where you need to come into alignment. Talk about your family values. Explore your blind spots. And strategize how to support one another.

PAIRINGS ❧

- Books: *Zen Meditations on Being a Mother* (with CD) by Roni Jay, *Momma Zen: Walking the Crooked Path of Motherhood* by Karen Maezen Miller, and *The Soul of Discipline* by Kim John Payne

journal on

Discipline

Reflect here on your approach
to discipline: Does it make you
feel good? Does it empower
your children? How effective is
your approach? Where does your
approach need more work? What
are some changes you'd like to try?

Rhythm

the heartbeat of home

By this time in your Sacred Motherhood *year, you are likely to be finding your groove. It is your groove, and no one else's, which means that you need to experiment and decide what truly works best for you. That said, we would like to offer a few simple words of wisdom: If you want to groove, you've got to have rhythm!*

YOU ❧

Rhythm preserves sanity. It frames the dance of life, synchronizing all of the different needs and desires that make family life either dynamic or chaotic. If everyone is pulling you in opposite directions, and you're faced with endless decisions about how to keep everyone on course, you could easily lose your mind! But a basic rhythm that weaves together your day, week, and year helps free your energy for joyful improvisation. For example, if your weekday afternoons follow a rhythm of quiet time, playtime, homework, and dinner prep, you'll know how to embrace a spontaneous tea party and still keep your evening void of exhaustion or bedlam.

Rhythm differs from routine—it builds energy to sustain itself, rather than draining energy through the dogged pursuit of an agenda. It asks that you pay attention to the heartbeat of your household—its optimal pace, its touchstone moments of connection, its periods of expansion and contraction, its sequences of activity that keep everything rolling—and honor this natural pulse to bring everyone and everything into coherence.

YOUR SOUL ❧

We are rhythmic beings. The heartbeat is the driving rhythm by which we live, yet we largely take it for granted. Moving out from the core, many rhythms support the vitality of our bodies and souls. The better we attend to these natural pulses, the more we can relax into the beat and be sustained by this exquisite design of energy movement.

Start by honing in on your breath, simply following the in-breath and the out-breath. Then, eventually, notice how you are not driving this life-breath but riding it into being. Then consider how the sun rises and sets to bookmark your daily rhythms of activity and rest without any effort on your part. What would it be like to wake up with the sun every morning? Could stepping outside each night to commune with Sister Moon make you more aware of your moods—creative, emotional, or reflective—in relationship to the waxing and waning of that luminous orb? Finally, how might seasonal rhythms of observation and celebration enrich your life with the energies unique to each time of year?

YOUR CHILD ⟋⟍

Children too thrive within a rhythmic home. In utero, your baby was entirely enveloped in the rhythm of your heartbeat. After birth, a baby's connection to the mother's rhythms continues to provide familiar comfort, and supports the baby in establishing breathing patterns and a regular heartbeat. Remaining close, even through the night, also promotes bonding and the beneficial synchronicity of mother-child sleep cycles.

As your children grow, you can continue to guide them in creating healthy life-rhythms. To varying degrees, all young children (and most of us mamas too) seek order in chaos, and appreciate knowing what comes next. If, for example, your household begins to unravel around bedtime, teeth-brushing battles might subside if everyone knows that the bedtime story will follow. Regular rhythm literally carries the moment, allowing you and your children to more naturally sink into relationship with one another and the world around you.

REFLECTIONS ⟋⟍

Joy arrives when you learn to live in the moment and greet whatever is present with appreciation and wonder. Layered rhythms can support you in doing this with more ease, turning daily life into a celebration. This week, try falling into step with the cycles of Earth and home. In doing so, you might guide your little ones on a wintry walk to discover crocuses peeking out from beneath the snow, and other signs that spring is just around the corner. Or you may find space to enjoy your morning coffee at the break of winter's slow-to-dawn days.

SACRED MOTHERHOOD PRACTICE ❧

LEARN A NEW RHYTHM. Choose just *one* thing that could bring more cadence and coherence to your home. Then give it a go! If it works like magic, you can add more. If it's a bomb, you'll know that you just dance to a different beat.

IDEAS ❧

- PICTURE YOUR IDEAL WEEKLY RHYTHM. Using the Beauty Way concept and some colored pencils or watercolors, bring your family's hours and days into synch with a visual aid. Get creative in representing how your week pulses with comings and goings, activities and downtime, spaciousness and overwhelm. Notice where it all comes together or falls apart. Then fine-tune your image until you like what you see.

- HONOR SEASONAL RHYTHMS. It is late winter now, so begin here. Create a family ritual to celebrate this transitional time and the coming thaw. Hold a "Farewell to Winter" party. Or make candles for the "Feast of Waxing Light," also known as Imbolc, a Celtic festival traditionally occurring at the beginning of February. With each new season, find special ways to align your family life with the Earth's annual journey around the sun.

PAIRINGS ❧

- Books: *Seven Times the Sun: Guiding Your Child through the Rhythms of the Day* by Shea Darian and *The Rhythm of Family: Discovering a Sense of Wonder Through the Seasons* by Amanda Blake Soule with Stephen Soule

What personal rhythms best support
you in your matrix of motherhood?

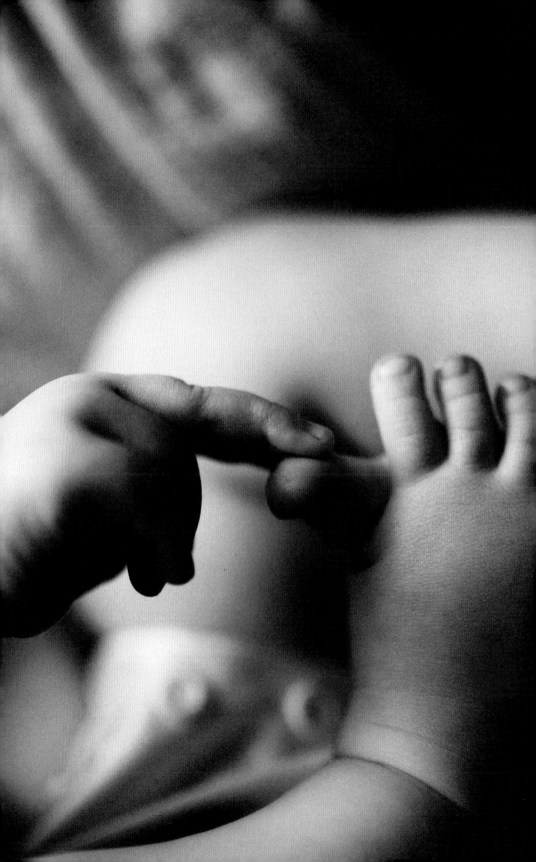

Love of Learning

a lifelong affair

No matter whwere you are on the path of Sacred Motherhood, *you have likely learned ample lessons about yourself and the art of mothering. Nevertheless, remember that motherhood is a* journey—*if ever you think you have arrived, you are missing the boat and setting off instead on a long, hard road. It's better to adopt a* lifelong *love of learning, so that you can embrace each new challenge or adventure with curiosity and wonder.*

YOU ☙

When it comes to the love of learning, you are your child's first and most influential teacher. You teach by example, so give some thought to how to "keep your game on." Obviously, you have delved into the mysteries of Sacred Motherhood with a willingness to feed your own unfolding as well as your children's. Now, as this sacred year winds down, what new terrain of motherhood piques your interest? What have you uncovered within yourself that calls for further exploration?

As mothers, we often think of our children as doing all the learning. They are young, after all, and can easily acquire a language, pick up an instrument, or join a sports team. But if you have always wanted to play the cello, and believe that ship has sailed, *think again!* Your willingness to be a beginner yourself is a priceless teaching for your children. They may lead you down some new trails as well. Never skied? Learn together. Motherhood is a never-ending *teachable moment.*

YOUR SOUL ☙

If any path in life defies mastery, it is motherhood. Just when you think you have the nap schedule figured out, it changes. And just when you are sure you thoroughly know your child, she becomes a teenager. Indeed, the more you learn, the less you know! By clinging to what you think you know, you are likely to overlook your most valuable life lessons. Chances are that your children are among your *greatest teachers.*

In "sacred-speak," prior to incarnating you signed up to learn specific lessons, and made agreements with other souls to share in a co-creative experience during this lifetime. Through both our light and our shadow, we nudge each other along in our souls' work. You can bet that the ways in which your children both inspire you and vex you are part of this grand plan. Likewise, you can rest assured that you are the *perfect* mother for your children because of—not in spite of—your imperfections as well as your gifts.

YOUR CHILD

From learning to ride a bike to choosing a path in life, your child's holistic development is a miracle that you have the honor to witness and support—but not direct. Resist the temptation to educate your children simply by filling them up with what you know. Rather, tap your child's own *inherent wisdom* and natural inquisitiveness by remembering the Latin root *educere*, "to draw out and lead forth."

How can you nurture the spirit of curiosity and instill the love of learning? Step outside and allow your child to discover that ice floats, or notice migrating birds stopping at your feeder. If your child expresses a keen interest in dress-up, follow that thread and make a trip to the children's theater. Make the most of every possible teachable moment. When a question arises, respond with, "I was wondering that too," or "Let's find out!"

REFLECTIONS

A wise elder once advised that when a teacher says, "I know," you should run in the opposite direction. When a teacher says, "I am learning," you are wise to listen. What kind of teacher do you want to be for your child?

SACRED MOTHERHOOD PRACTICE

BECOME A STUDENT. This week, commit to one new path of learning for yourself. Pay attention to where you feel the tug of new growth, or sense you are being held back by a lack of know-how. Buy a book, sign up for a class, or fling open the doors of experimentation. Never stop loving or learning!

IDEAS ⟳

- START A FAMILY-DINNER ROUND TABLE. Once a week, have each member of the family step into the role of teacher by making a short presentation about something they know and love. Make it casual, and keep it fun!

- REFLECT ON YOUR CHILDREN'S EDUCATION, AND DISCUSS IT WITH YOUR PARTNER. For this exercise, be open-minded and idealistic—the sky's the limit! What are your philosophies and ideals? Are your children's educational pathways feeding their love of learning? What educational options are available in your community? How can you manifest your highest vision of education for your children?

PAIRINGS ⟳

- Books: *You Are Your Child's First Teacher: Encouraging Your Child's Natural Development from Birth to Age Six* by Rahima Baldwin Dancy and *Beyond the Rainbow Bridge: Nuturing Our Children from Birth to Seven* by Barbara J. Patterson and Pamela Bradley

- Cards: *Grimm's Animal ABC Waldorf Alphabet Cards: Artistic Watercolor Letter Cards in English with Ideas for Playing* by Grimm's Spieland Holz Design

Love of Learning

Describe some of the most important learning experiences of your
life. How did they come about? Were they planned, or unexpected?
Did these experiences become turning points in your life? How might
they play into the unfolding of your soul's work?

_____

_____

_____

_____

_____

_____

_____

_____

_____

_____

_____

_____

_____

_____

_____

_____

Empowerment

your presence is your power

In the depth of winter, you need to be reminded of your strength. The mention of winter may conjure dreary images of drifted snow and diving temperatures, or bleak memories of long days and sleepless nights. Either way, winter hardships equate with survival mode. Fear not! This week we tap a wellspring of POWER that can help you weather even the toughest storms.

YOU ⟡

There is no denying that motherhood puts your powers to the test. There are times when you are powerful beyond belief—when giving birth, defending your children, or mustering patience at the end of a trying day. But there are times when you feel powerless in the face of mothering's trials and tribulations, whether bothersome tantrums or heartbreaking traumas.

What does it take for you to feel fully anchored in your seat of power through all of this? Do you need to post affirmations around the house to remind yourself that you've got what it takes? Leave an uplifting message for yourself on your bathroom mirror or phone screen. Do you need others to reflect your light when the gloom settles and you lose sight of your own radiance? Get your partner or a friend on board, and make a pact to do this for each other.

Your empowered life will flower when you know how to pull yourself up whenever you fall down. It will bloom when you are truly *seen* and *loved* by yourself and others.

YOUR SOUL ⟡

In Vajrayana Buddhism, before you begin a new practice you must receive an "empowerment," which reveals to you some aspect of the enlightened mind that is associated with a particular deity. The empowerment ritual serves to transform your ordinary, conditional way of seeing, so that you may perceive the pure BUDDHA NATURE that resides within you and everyone.

Activating your SACRED PERCEPTION can be empowering in your practice of motherhood as well. What if you could recognize that power naturally arises when you open to your essential nature? Can you stop striving and pushing yourself and others, and sapping your energy through agitation and frustration? Can you trust the mysterious power of stillness at the heart of your very presence?

Close your eyes, and bring your awareness into that deep space of silent knowing and inexplicable contentment. Herein lies your TRUE POWER. This power enables you to engage and inspire your children. It is a magnetic, grounding, and majestic force—a power like that of a mountain.

YOUR CHILD ☙

Sometimes we can see the TRUE POWER in ourselves, and sometimes we need others to hold up a mirror. You can do this for your child. Mirroring for empowerment is the simple and powerful act of reflecting back to your child the strength and beauty and gifts that you recognize in them. In essence you are saying, *"I see you!"* And you do not see just your child's dirty face or mismatched socks. You see the divine seed inside, and you name it: "I notice how much love and care you extend to your friends. You have an enormous heart, and delight in sharing it with others." This simple moment of acknowledgment will encourage the growth of the light and power inside your child.

REFLECTIONS ☙

Being seen is deeply nourishing. When you commit to truly see another person in their highest expression, the act of mirroring feeds your loving essence as well. You cannot attach conditions or manipulations to empowerment; they will not stick. If your mirroring is slightly off, it will not ring true—but no harm is done, because your intentions are pure. As you practice over time, however, you will hone your ability to see and reflect the precious jewels that we each embody in our own unique way.

SACRED MOTHERHOOD PRACTICE ⌒◦

BECOME AN INSTRUMENT OF TRUE POWER. Each day, commit to beholding and reflecting the divinity of one other being. Don't hold back! Through the beauty you see and the beauty you speak, the whole world becomes more sacred. And in serving as a mirror of all this beauty, you become even more beautiful yourself.

IDEAS ⌒◦

· CREATE AN EMPOWERMENT RITUAL. Choose a guest of honor—a sister, a friend, or a relative—and invite others to bring a symbolic gift and eloquent words that mirror the beauty and power of this dear one. This ritual creates a special love fest to power up a birthday, a Blessing Way ceremony, or a First Moon (menarche) celebration. But don't feel you have to wait for a special occasion. Every day is a good day for EMPOWERMENT!

· GO TO THE BOWL. This Sacred Living Movement tradition centers on a bountiful bowl of bath salts. The bowl is passed around a circle of women. Each sister adds her gift (essential oils, dried flowers, herbs, etc.) to the bowl and proclaims *out loud* her intentions for living an empowered life. Everyone takes some of the embellished, empowered bath salts home, and uses them to steep herself in the collective power of being witnessed in sisterhood.

PAIRINGS ⌒◦

· Crystal: Lapis lazuli is a powerful stone for supporting your personal power and spiritual journey. It works with both the third-eye and throat chakras, to stimulate both self-awareness and self-expression.

Empowerment

Use this space to write down all that you want to EMPOWER in your life. What is your true nature, and how does this manifest in you as a powerful woman and mama? What enlightened aspects of yourself do you want to cultivate? What dreams do you want to feed?

_____

_____

_____

_____

_____

_____

_____

_____

_____

_____

_____

_____

_____

_____

_____

The Gift

bringing home the boon

You've come a long way, Mama! Remember all the way back in Week 1? You heard a call and answered it, embarking on the journey of SACRED MOTHER-HOOD. *With courage and curiosity, you have explored the depths and heights of what it means to be a mother. Along the way you have, we hope, gathered a few riches. Now it is time to* BRING HOME THE BOON.

YOU ❧

On a mythic journey, the boon is the gift that a hero (or heroine) claims and brings back as an offering to his (or her) people. The gift is not something newly discovered, but something forgotten or lost that is remembered or retrieved. In some stories, there are demons to slay or deserts to cross. In others, the light of love exposes the sought-after pearl. No matter what the journey entails, the gift ultimately symbolizes a return to the hero's deepest *truth*.

This week, pause and reflect on the journey of Sacred Motherhood: What inner demons have you slain this year? What harsh landscapes have you successfully traversed in meeting the needs of your children? What has your love unearthed? And what gift have you recovered?

Perhaps the boon is something that you lost track of in motherhood, then found anew. Or maybe it is a treasure you have carried all along, but only recently have come to value. As you have courageously walked the mystical and mundane path of motherhood, have you been chipping away at your tired but tenacious beliefs and patterns? Are you now ready to delve into the mystery of who you are, and reveal your true *radiance*?

YOUR SOUL ❧

At the beginning of this sacred year, you answered the call to Sacred Motherhood, and set an intention with an "I AM" statement about the wise, empowered mother you have always been *and* were yet to become. This is your GIFT—and now is the moment to complete that process of claiming it, and come home to yourself and your people bearing the riches you have gathered on your journey in these past months.

As you approach the final threshold of claiming and giving away these gifts, you may encounter obstacles that block you from seeing your truth and owning the pearl that is your gift. Take a moment to consider: Is there anything keeping you from stepping into your power? Are you clinging to old beliefs, roles, wounds, addictions, or fears? Delve into your psyche, and shine some light on anything still lurking in the shadows. Now, when you imagine truly letting all of that go, what are you ready to *claim* as your gift to yourself, your children, and the world?

YOUR CHILD ☙

Each child is born with a gift. It is as if a sparkly, heavenly treasure were placed into the cradle alongside every newborn. This treasure is inseparable from the child; it is not something that must be found or attained. In fact, it often comes so easily that it may be dismissed or underappreciated. Or a child may be afraid to let others see that most precious pearl hidden deep within.

As a mother, you have the honor of beholding this gift. *Sing* to it, *pray* for it, and *welcome* it. Realize that you may not understand or even perceive the full spectrum of its never-before-seen beauty. Don't put it in your box of expectations or unlived dreams. Instead, delight in its spiraling expression, and nurture it with your unconditional love and patient offerings of *beauty*.

REFLECTIONS ☙

Your gift is like a glowing ember. Once kindled, it will not go out. It only asks that you feed it, and share its warmth and light with the world. Although your year of Sacred Motherhood may be coming to an end, continue tending this inner flame by letting go of perfection and firing up your passions. Each day, do one thing that stokes your inner flame. And remember, *gifts are for giving!*

SACRED MOTHERHOOD PRACTICE ⌒

BRING HOME THE BOON. Find or make a beautiful power object that represents the gift you are claiming. Then set aside some time for yourself in nature or some other sacred space. Hold your power object close to your heart, imbuing it with your soul-fire. Place it on your altar, and commit to feeding it each day with your prayers, your songs, or your actions.

IDEAS ⌒

- LET IT GO. Create a ceremony to release whatever might be holding you back from claiming your gift. Write down everything that you are ready to give up in order to own your full power. Speak your list *out loud,* and then throw it into the fire, bury it in the earth, or surrender it to the water. Let these grandmother elements bear away whatever no longer serves you.

- GIVE YOUR GIFT. Identify one significant thing that you can do this week, to share your gift with others. You could take action on a dream or vision, speak your truth to a loved one, or do something special with your child. In carrying this out, what challenges might arise? How are you going to honor your gift while staying in your POWER?

PAIRING ⌒

- Book: *Creative Inspirations: Art Activity Pages to Relax and Enjoy!* by Design Originals

- Music: "I Am the Light of My Soul" by Snatam Kaur, and "Let It Go" by Idina Menzel

journal on

The Gift

What is your gift? If your life were an expression of this gift, how would it be different than it is now? What would you be doing? How would you be feeling? And, finally, what gifts have you received from your year of *Sacred Motherhood?* How are you going to continue stoking your soul-fire on the path of motherhood, and radiating your love and light?

_____

_____

_____

_____

_____

_____

_____

_____

_____

_____

_____

_____

SACRED LIVING MOVEMENT RESOURCES

The Sacred Living Movement started with a book, a vision, and a dream. Anni Daulter wrote *Sacred Pregnancy* and held a retreat in November of 2012 to train visionary birth-workers how to "hold space" for birthing mothers to shift pregnancy and birth from a medicalized experience to something honored and sacred.

After that flagship retreat, the movement grew into more programs and ideas, and has become a grand vision that we now call the Sacred Living Movement. We quickly realized that all aspects of the life journey needed to be addressed, honored, marked, and seen as sacred, so we started developing programs to fit the needs of the communities we were serving.

Today we have traveled to over nine different countries, trained nearly 1,000 women to be Sacred Pregnancy Instructors, and expanded who we are and who we want to be by including more classes and retreats that support living a truly Sacred Life. We now offer many live and online trainings to enhance your life and/or become certified to either teach or offer direct services in your own community. If this movement interests you, please see our list below and visit our websites.

· Sacred Living Movement (main website): www.sacredliving movement.com
· Sacred Living Movement University: www.sacredlivinguniversity .com
· Sacred Motherhood: www.sacred-motherhood.com

- Sacred Pregnancy: www.sacred-pregnancy.com
- Sacred Postpartum: www.sacredpostpartum.net
- Sacred Beginnings (for mom and baby): www.sacred-beginning.com
- Sacred Relationship (for couples): www.oursacredrelationship.com
- I AM Sisterhood: www.iamsisterhood.com
- Sacred Ayurveda: www.sacred-ayurveda.com
- Sacred Essence (natural family living): www.sacred-essence.com
- Sacred Sweeties (for little girls and their moms): www.sacredsweeties.com
- Sacred Moon Daughters (for girls coming of age): www.sacredmoondaughters.com
- Sacred Menopause: www.sacred-menopause.com
- Sacred Sons: www.sacred-sons.com
- Sacred Men: www.sacredmen.com
- Sacred Fertility: www.sacredfertility.com
- Sacred Birth Journey (for couples): www.sacred-birthjourney.com
- Sacred Midwife: www.sacredmidwife.com
- Sacred Doula: www.sacreddoula.com
- Sacred Milk: www.sacred-milk.com
- Sacred Loss: www.sacred-loss.com
- Sacred Medicine Woman: www.sacred-medicinewoman.com
- Sacred Yoga: www.sacredyoga.net
- Sacred Biz: www.sacred-biz.com

Additional Sacred Living Movement Mini-Programs
(see www.sacredlivingmovement.com)

- Sacred Year with Anni Daulter
- Sacred Self Love
- Sacred Mother Blessing
- Sacred Crystals
- Sacred Healing Birth Trauma
- Sacred Scent
- Sacred Art
- Sacred Tarot
- Sacred Baby Feet (Reflexology)
- Sacred Scent for Birth-Workers
- Sacred Blood Mysteries
- Celtic Wheel
- Sacred Medicine Cabinet
- Sacred Moon Mysteries
- Sacred Detox
- Sacred Belly Bind
- Sacred Tea
- Sacred Birth Dance
- Sacred Sisterhood Circles
- Sacred Mentor
- Sacred Book Intentions
- Sacred V-Steams
- Sacred Red Drum
- Awakening the Heart
- Sacred Wild Woman

Other International Sacred Living Movement Websites:

- Sacred Living Movement Canada: www.sacredlivingcanada.com
- Sacred Living Movement UK: www.sacredlivinguk.com

ACKNOWLEDGMENTS

Special thanks to everyone involved at North Atlantic Books: Tim McKee, for your guidance and vision; Vanessa Ta and Emily Boyd for your hard work on all the details and your support; and Susan Bumps, for believing in the book and this sacred mission. Thank you, Claudia Smelser for your beauty way design of this book, it's gorgeous! To all of the incredible photographers who put their work forward in this book with openness and love, this book would not be the same without you. And to Jade Beall, for the cover photo—your work inspires and captivates us deeply, and we are so blessed to be able to share this image with the world. Thank you all!

I am deeply blessed to have so many amazing people around me, and while I could spend all day and night thanking all of them, I have to pare it down to this list! Firstly, I must thank my sacred babies, Zoe, Lotus, Bodhi, and River, and my husband, Tim. You all teach me to be the best version of myself, and for that I am forever grateful. I love you all more than there are stars in the sky. Thank you to my own mother, and my in-laws, Bonnie and Dan Walter for all of their continued love and support. Niki Dewart, you inspire me, and I am so delighted that you were willing to take this journey with me. I could not be happier with the birth of our amazing book.

To my sisterhood of women who support me and the Sacred Living Movement vision: Sue Crowder, Alyssa Wood-Tozzi, Jessica Booth, Tnah Louise, Jessica Smithson, Sarah Dexter, Sara Harkness, Katie Mullins, Nina Lee, Sara Goff, Lorie McCoy, Amanda Omoth, Kiera Lillesve, Austin Rees, Radha Schwaller, Jacqueline

Pace, Kerry Stokes, Kristin Revere , Leia Swanberg, Corinne Laan, Myrriah Raimbault, Stephanie Green, Debbie Armour, Caroline Lyons, Carley Allen, Tree Charles, Kim Graham-Nye, Hayley Warren Lane , Peyton Callahan, Errin Proper, Lety Murphy, Megan Kibling, and Myriam Pearson-Martinez—I love you all deeply.

Lastly, but not least, thank you to my own mother, who showed me that strength of heart is the most important attribute a person can have—and who taught me how to be a great mom. I love you. —*Anni*

My heartfelt gratitude to my beloved husband, Steve Dewart, for doing this sacred dance alongside me and loving me through it all, and to our children, Haven, Afton, and Story, who are my muses and true joy. To my circle of mothers: Janet Beurskens, for arriving at the eleventh hour so that I could sneak off to finish writing this book; Carolyn Clark, for her tenderness and playfulness; and especially my own mother, Karen Richards, for her deep heart and unwavering devotion to our whole family. To my father, Don Richards, for teaching me to believe in myself. To my sister, Gwen Scherer, whose dedication and perseverance as a mother inspires me to no end.

To my soul sisters: Amanda Botur, Tara Brockman, Laurie Dean, Lindsay Heppner, Ashley Johnson, Erin Jospe, Micki Kibler, Erin Kott, Alison Litchfield, Melanie MacKinnon, Jen Malcom, Elizabeth Marglin, Alison Nacht, Ruth Wharton, and Erin Witbeck, whose wisdom and sisterhood has guided me down the path of Sacred Motherhood. To my children's teachers, Perky Hubner, Kaivalya Miller, Sandra Haber, and Lynn St. Pierre, for tending my children's minds, bodies, and spirits.

And, finally, to Anni, for her generosity of spirit and Beauty Way— it has been a pure pleasure and an honor to create this with you. Thank you for bringing this book and me into the Sacred Living Movement. —*Niki*

Index

ABOUT THE AUTHORS

Anni Daulter

ANNI DAULTER is the author of *Sacred Pregnancy* (North Atlantic 2012) and is the founder of the Sacred Living Movement. She travels the world leading retreats that inspire, uplift, and connect women in many areas of their lives. She trains birth workers to lead Sacred Pregnancy classes, helps couples heal at Sacred Relationship retreats, empowers women at I AM Sisterhood retreats, and brings moms and daughters together in celebration at Sacred Sweeties retreats. Anni has written six other books to inspire natural family living, and is an artist of the Beauty Way. She ventures a high-vibration lifestyle with her husband, Tim, and her four children, Zoë, Lotus Sunshine, Bodhi, and River.

Kirsten Boyer Photography

NIKI DEWART is an author and rites-of-passage guide devoted to walking the sacred path of motherhood. Over the past twenty years, she has studied countless spiritual traditions and traveled worldwide to sit with wisdom keepers. In 2005, Niki began a lifetime's work with her true gurus—her children. She now writes books and leads rituals, workshops, and retreats that nurture the soul of mothering. Niki is coauthor of *The Mother's Wisdom Deck* (Sterling 2012) and offers Sacred Motherhood trainings and retreats as a leader in the Sacred Living Movement. She is also a founder of Applesong, a pioneering cottage school that nourishes the bodies, minds, and spirits of children in her community. She lives a meaning-rich family life with her beloved partner, Steve, and their three children, Haven, Afton, and Story.

Please visit Anni and Niki at www.SacredLivingMovement.com and www.Sacred-Motherhood.com

ABOUT THE PHOTOGRAPHY

Many photographers shared their beautiful, visionary work with us to make *Sacred Motherhood* the best book it could possibly be. We are in deep gratitude for their work, and want to thank them all so much for sharing with us. A special thanks to Jade Beall, Trevor Mars of SoulMakes, Lupen Grainne, Camilla Albano-Fotografia, The Visionary Photographic Art of Chanel Baran, The Blissful Maven, and Megan Kibling-Elizondo, for giving so freely of your creative work.

SPRING

Spring opening main photo—"Rose Mandala"
Lupen Grainne Photography, www.etsy.com/shop/lupengrainne

Spring opening photo—"Meditating Pregnant Goddess"
Melissa Jean, www.melissajean.com.au

Spring opening photo—"Mama and Baby"
Camilla Albano-Fotografia, www.flickr.com/photos/camilla_albano

Week 1—The Call
Melissa Jean, www.melissajean.com.au

Week 2—Birth

Rae Marie Photography, www.raemarie.com.au

Week 3—Mindful Mothering

Megan Kibling-Elizondo, Nutmeg Photography, www.nutmegphotos
.smugmug.com

Week 4—Mother Love

Camilla Albano-Fotografia, www.flickr.com/photos/camilla_albano

Week 5—Sacred Feminine

Jade Beall, www.jadebeall.com

Week 6—Creativity
Sari Mattsson, www.sarimattsson.com

Week 7—The Inner Flame
Kiera Lillesve, www.kieralillesvefoto.com

Week 8—Do it with JOY
Camilla Albano-Fotografia, www.flickr.com/photos/camilla_albano

Week 9—ImPERFECTion
Heidi Marie Wagstaff, www.truefeather.net

Week 10—Sacred YES + Holy NO
Heidi Marie Wagstaff, www.truefeather.net

Week 11—Wild Motherhood
The Visionary Photographic Art of Chanel Baran, www.chanelbaran.com

Week 12—Adventure
Brandi Johnson, Kindred Photographer, www.kindredphotographer.com

Week 13—Animal Guides

SUMMER

Summer opening main photo—"Summer Picnic"
Soulmakes, www.soulmakes.com

Summer opening photo—"Fire"
Katy Leet, www.katyleetphotography.com

Summer opening photo—"Spark of a Girl"
The Blissful Maven, www.theblissfulmaven.com

Summer opening photo—"Kantha Flag"
Soulmakes, www.soulmakes.com

Week 14—Trust
Paulina Splechta, www.paulinasplechta.com

Week 15—Embodiment
The Visionary Photographic Art of Chanel Baran, www.chanelbaran.com;
model: Nehanda Nyaanda Rusere

Week 16—The Beauty Way
Heidi Marie Wagstaff, www.truefeather.net

Week 17—Nurture
The Visionary Photographic Art of Chanel Baran, www.chanelbaran.com

Week 18—Sacred Play
Chelsea Brooke Roisum, www.cbrphotography.ca

Week 19—Get Dirty
Tnah Louise, Bella Faccia Foto, www.bellafacciafoto.com

Week 20—Two Hands
Soulmakes, www.soulmakes.com

Week 21—Simplicity
Camilla Albano-Fotografia, www.flickr.com/photos/camilla_albano

Week 22—Patience
The Visionary Photographic Art of Chanel Baran, www.chanelbaran.com

Week 23 —Tears + Fears
Kara May Photography, www.karamayphotography.com

Week 24—Losing It
Kiera Lillesve, www.kieralillesvefoto.com; model: Jessica Lauren

Week 25—Body as Temple
The Visionary Photographic Art of Chanel Baran, www.chanelbaran.com

Week 26—Sacred Relationship
The Blissful Maven, www.theblissfulmaven.com

FALL

Fall opening main photo—"Fall Still Life"
Lupen Grainne Photography, www.etsy.com/shop/lupengrainne

Fall opening photo—"Kale Squash Salad"
Anna Pettigrew, www.annapettigrew.com

Fall opening photo—"Mom and Daughter Cuddle"
Heidi Marie Wagstaff, www.truefeather.net

Fall opening photo—"Spices"
Katy Leet, www.katyleetphotography.com

Week 27—Walking Your Path
Kristina Belkina, www.kristinabelkina.com; model: Nikiah Seeds at www
.redmoonmysteryschool.com

Week 28—Intuition
The Visionary Photographic Art of Chanel Baran, www.chanelbaran.com

Week 29—Soulmates
Lovebirds: Megan Gasiorowski and Tony Viton

Week 30—Nest
"Mama Feeding Alba" by Nirrimi Firebrace, www.fireandjoy.com

Week 31—Nourish
Katy Leet, www.katyleetphotography.com

Week 32—Sacred Earth
Camilla Albano-Fotografia, www.flickr.com/photos/camilla_albano

Week 33—Healing
Megan Kibling-Elizondo, Nutmeg Photography, www.nutmegphotos
.smugmug.com

Week 34—Forgiveness
Camilla Albano-Fotografia, www.flickr.com/photos/camilla_albano

Week 35—Storytelling
Lupen Grainne Photography, www.etsy.com/shop/lupengrainne

Week 36—Dreamtime
Heidi Marie Wagstaff, www.truefeather.net

Week 37—Shadow + Light
Camilla Albano-Fotografia, www.flickr.com/photos/camilla_albano

Week 38—Passages
Chelsea Brooke Roisum, www.cbrphotography.ca

Week 39—Gratitude + Abundance
Ivette Ivens Photography, www.ivetteivens.com

WINTER

Winter opening main photo—"The Gift"
Megan Kibling-Elizondo, Nutmeg Photography, www.nutmegphotos
.smugmug.com

Winter opening photo—"Incense"
Kiera Lillesve, www.kieralillesvefoto.com

Winter opening photo—"Tea and Feathers"
Sari Mattsson, www.sarimattsson.com

Winter opening photo—"Mom and Baby"
The Blissful Maven, www.theblissfulmaven.com

Week 40—Celebration
Soulmakes, www.soulmakes.com

Week 41—Loving Kindness
Lisa Pedersen Photography; models: Sian Marie Pilkington and Baby Hazel Rose

Week 42—Breaking Bread
Megan Kibling-Elizondo, Nutmeg Photography, www.nutmegphotos .smugmug.com

Week 43—Family
Pearl Oz, www.vintageprettypearl.blogspot.com

Week 44—Sisterhood
Megan Kibling-Elizondo, Nutmeg Photography, www.nutmegphotos .smugmug.com

Week 45—Connection
Michelle Craig, Michelle Craig Photography, www.2pedalsphotography.com; models: Jessica Lauren and Baby Nico Luna Lewis

Week 46—Superpowers
Soulmakes, www.soulmakes.com

Week 47—Speaking + Listening
Ashley Johnson

Week 48—Discipline
The Blissful Maven, www.theblissfulmaven.com

Week 49—Rhythm
Lola Brown, www.lifeinanalogue.com; model: Jude Harkness

Week 50—Love of Learning
The Blissful Maven, www.theblissfulmaven.com

Week 51—Empowerment
The Blissful Maven, www.theblissfulmaven.com

Week 52—The Gift
Megan Kibling-Elizondo, Nutmeg Photography, www.nutmegphotos .smugmug.com